# NOT THAT KIND OF GIRL

*A Young Woman Tells You What
She's "Learned"*

## Lena Dunham

FOURTH ESTATE·*London*

Fourth Estate
An imprint of HarperCollins*Publishers*
77–85 Fulham Palace Road,
Hammersmith, London W6 8JB
www.4thestate.co.uk

First published in Great Britain in 2014 by Fourth Estate

First published in the United States in 2014 by Random House,
an imprint and division of Random House LLC,
a Penguin Random House Company, New York.

2

Lena Dunham asserts the moral right to be identified as the author of this work

*Not That Kind of Girl* is a work of nonfiction.
Some names and identifying details have been changed.

Illustrations by Joana Avillez
Book design by Elizabeth Spiridakis Olson

A catalogue record for this book is available from the British Library

ISBN HB 978-0-00-810126-8
ISBN TPB 978-0-00-751552-3

Printed and bound in Great Britain by Clays Ltd, St Ives plc

**MIX**
Paper from
responsible sources
FSC® C007454

Find out more about HarperCollins and the environment at
**www.harpercollins.co.uk/green**

For my family, of course.

For Nora.

And for Jack,
who is just as she said he would be.

*Deep in her soul, however, she was waiting for something to happen. Like a sailor in distress, she would gaze out over the solitude of her life with desperate eyes, seeking some white sail in the mists of the far-off horizon. She did not know what this chance event would be, what wind would drive it to her, what shore it would carry her to, whether it was a longboat or a three-decked vessel, loaded with anguish or filled with happiness up to the portholes. But each morning, when she awoke, she hoped it would arrive that day. . . .*

—GUSTAVE FLAUBERT, *Madame Bovary*


*How quickly you transform the energy life throws you into folded bows of art.*

—MY FATHER, admonishing me

# *Contents*

# *Introduction*

I AM TWENTY years old and I hate myself. My hair, my face, the curve of my stomach. The way my voice comes out wavering and my poems come out maudlin. The way my parents talk to me in a slightly higher register than they talk to my sister, as if I'm a government worker that's snapped and, if pushed hard enough, might blow up the hostages I've got tied up in my basement.

I cover up this hatred with a kind of aggressive self-acceptance. I dye my hair a fluorescent shade of yellow, cutting it into a mullet more inspired by photos of 1980s teen mothers than by any current beauty trend. I dress in neon spandex that hugs in all the wrong places. My mother and I have a massive fight when I choose to wear a banana-printed belly shirt and pink leggings to the Vatican and religious tourists gawk and turn away.

I'm living in a dormitory that was, not too long ago, an old-age home for low-income townspeople and I don't like thinking about where they might be now. My roommate has moved to New York to explore farm-to-fork cooking and lesbianism, so I'm alone, in a ground-floor one-bedroom, a fact I relish until one night a female rugby player rips my screen door off the hinges and barges into the dorm to attack her philandering girlfriend. I've bought a VHS player and a pair of knitting needles and spend most nights on the sofa, making half a scarf for a boy I like who had a manic break and dropped out. I've made two short films, both of which my father deemed "interesting but beside the point," and am so paralyzed as a writer that I've started translating poems from languages I don't speak, some kind of Surrealist exercise meant to inspire me but also prevent me from thinking the perverse, looping thoughts that come unbidden: I am hideous. I am going to be living in a mental hospital by the time I am twenty-nine. I will never amount to anything.

You wouldn't know it to see me at a party. In a crowd I am recklessly cheerful, dressed to the nines in thrift-shop gowns and press-on fingernails, fighting the sleepiness that comes from the 350 milligrams of medication I take every night. I dance the hardest, laugh the hardest at my own jokes, and make casual reference to my vagina, like it's a car or a chest of drawers. I got mono last year, but it never really went away. Occasionally, one of my glands blows up to the size of a golf ball and protrudes from my neck like one of the bolts that keep Frankenstein's monster intact.

I have friends: a kind group of girls whose passions (baking, pressing flowers, community organizing) do not stir me. I feel guilt about this, a sense that my inability to be at home with them proves, once and for all, that I am no good. I laugh, I agree, I find reasons to go home early. I have the nagging sense that my *true* friends are waiting for me, beyond college, unusual women whose ambitions are as big as their past transgressions, whose hair is piled high, dramatic like topiaries at Versailles, and who never, ever say "too much information" when you mention a sex dream you had about your father.

But that's also how I felt in high school, sure that *my* people were from elsewhere and going elsewhere and that they would recognize me when they saw me. They would like me enough that it wouldn't matter if I liked myself. They would see the good in me so that I could, too.

🍎

On Saturdays my friends and I load into somebody's old Volvo and head to a thrift store, where we buy tchotchkes that reek of other people's lives and clothes that we believe will enhance our own. We all want to look like characters on the sitcoms of our youth, the teenagers we admired when we were still kids. None of the pants ever fit me, unless I head into the maternity section, so I buy mostly sacklike dresses and Cosby sweaters.

Some days, my haul is massive: a peach power suit with subtle coffee stains, leggings with trompe l'oeil chains running down the sides, a pair of boots specially made for someone with legs of different lengths. But some days the spread is meager. The usual bounty of patterned off-brand Keds and ripped negligees has been snapped up. On one such day, I wander over to the book section, where people discard their guides to better divorce and crafting how-tos, sometimes even their scrapbooks and family photo albums.

I scan the dusty shelf, which looks like the book collection of an unhappy and maybe even illiterate family. I ignore get-rich-quick advice, stop briefly at Miss Piggy's autobiography, contemplate a book called *Sisters: The Gift of Love*. But when I reach a faded paperback with edges so yellowed they have almost gone green, I stop. *Having It All*, by Helen Gurley Brown, who graces her own cover, leaning against her tidy desk in the kind of shoulder-padded plum suit I have taken to wearing ironically, all pearls and knowing smile.

I spend the sixty-five cents required to take the book home. In the car I show it to my friends like it's a decorative joke, something for my shelf of kitschy trophies and Sears photo-studio shots of strangers' kids. This is our hobby, appropriating meaningful artifacts and displaying them as evidence of who we will never be. But I know I'm going to devour this book, and when I get home I head straight to bed, shivering under my patchwork quilt, an Ohio snowstorm swirling in the parking lot outside my window.

The book is from 1982, and on the inside cover is an inscription, written in ballpoint pen: "To Betty! Love, Margaret, your Optifast friend. ☺" This moves me, the idea that the book was handed from one woman to another in some long-ago weight-loss support group. I extend her message in my mind: *Betty, we can do it. We* are *doing it. Let this book take you to the stars and beyond.*

I race home from class every day for a week to devour Helen's teachings. I'm electrified by the way that, in *Having It All*, Gurley Brown shares her assorted humiliations and occasional triumphs and explains, with Idiot's Guide precision, how you too can be blessed with "love, success, sex, money, even if you're starting with nothing."

Most of her advice, it should be noted, is

absolutely bananas. She encourages readers to eat fewer than a thousand calories a day ("crashing is okay, so is fasting . . . Satisfied is out of the question. You have to feel slightly uncomfortable and hungry during your weight loss or it probably isn't happening"), avoid having children if you possibly can, and be blow job ready at all times ("the more sex you have, the more you can tolerate"). Helen has little tolerance for free will in this department: "Exhaustion, preoccupation with a problem, menstrual cramps—nothing is a good excuse for not making love unless you happen to be so angry with the man in your bed your eyes are darting around their sockets and your teeth are grinding."

Some of her advice is a little more reasonable: "Always leave for the airport fifteen minutes earlier than you *could*. It will save your valves wearing out," or "If you have severe personal problems then I think you go to a shrink for advice and support. I can no more imagine not going to get your hurting head and *heart* taken care of than one would go around the streets with blood spurting out of your throat . . ." But her frank wisdom loses some of its power because it's forced to occupy the same space as gems such as "to me, avoiding married men totally when you're single would be like passing up first aid in a Tijuana hospital when you're bleeding to death because you prefer an immaculate American hospital some unreachable distance across the border."

*Having It All* is divided into sections, each section a journey into some usually sacrosanct aspect of feminine life such as diet, sex, or the intricacies of marriage. But despite her demented theories, which jibe not even a little bit with my distinctly feminist upbringing, I appreciate the way Helen shares her own embarrassing, acne-ridden history in an attempt to say *Look, happiness and satisfaction can happen to anyone.* In the process she reveals her own unique pathos (a passage about binge eating baklava stands out in my mind), but maybe I underestimated her. Maybe that is not an accident but is, in fact, her gift.

When I found her book, I did not yet understand Helen Gurley Brown's position in the canon, that she had been written about and reacted to by the women who would come to guide me, women like Gloria Steinem and Nora Ephron. I did not know that she was the bane of both the women's movement and the smut-police, or that she was still alive and in her late eighties, still peddling her particular brand of chipper, oblivious help for the downtrodden. All I knew was that she painted a picture of a life made much richer by having once been, as she calls it, a *Mouseburger:* unpretty, unspecial, unformed. She believed that, ultimately, Mouseburgers are the women who will triumph, having lived to tell the tale of being overlooked and underloved. Hers is a self-serving perspective, but one I needed more than anything. Maybe, as Helen preached, a powerful, confident, and, yes, even sexy woman could be made, not born. Maybe.

There is nothing gutsier to me than a person announcing that their story is one that deserves to be told, especially if that person is a woman. As hard as we have worked and as far as we have come, there are still so many forces conspiring to tell women that our concerns are petty, our opinions aren't needed, that we lack the gravitas necessary for our stories to matter. That personal writing by women is no more than an exercise in vanity and that we should appreciate this new world for women, sit down, and shut up.

But I want to tell my stories and, more than that, I *have to* in order to stay sane: stories about waking up to my adult fe-

male body and being disgusted and terrified. About getting
my butt touched at an internship, having to prove myself in a
meeting full of fifty-year-old men, and going to a black-tie
event with the crustiest red nose you ever saw. About allowing
myself to be treated by men in ways I knew were wrong. Stories about my mother, my grandmother, the first guy I loved
who turned semi-gay, and the first girl I loved who turned
into my enemy. And if I could take what I've learned and
make one menial job easier for you, or prevent you from having the kind of sex where you feel you must keep your sneakers on in case you want to run away during the act, then every
misstep of mine was worthwhile. I'm already predicting my
future shame at thinking I had anything to offer you, but also
my future glory in having stopped you from trying an expen-
sive juice cleanse or thinking that it was your fault when the
person you are dating suddenly backs away, intimidated by
the clarity of your personal mission here on earth. No, I am
not a sexpert, a psychologist, or a dietitian. I am not a mother
of three or the owner of a successful hosiery franchise. But I
am a girl with a keen interest in having it all, and what follows
are hopeful dispatches from the frontlines of that struggle.

# SECTION I
# *Love & Sex*

# *Take My Virginity*
## *(No, Really, Take It)*

WHEN I WAS NINE, I wrote a vow of celibacy on a piece of paper and ate it. I promised myself, in orange Magic Marker, that I would remain a virgin until I graduated from high school. This seemed important because I knew my mother had waited until the summer before college and also because Angela Chase seemed pretty messed up by her experience at that flophouse where high school kids went to copulate. If my relationship to liver pâté was any indication—and I had recently eaten so much that I barfed—then my willpower left much to be desired. I would need something stronger than resolve to prevent me from having intercourse too early in life, so I wrote the vow up and asked my mother to sign the document. She refused. "You just don't know what life will bring, and I don't want you feeling guilty," she said.

Ultimately, the contract was an unnecessary precaution. The opportunity never arose in high school, nor even during my first year of college at the New School, unless you count a near miss with a stocky, aspiring pilot named James. Though never consummated, that encounter went far enough that I had to fish a mint-colored, never-used condom out from behind my dormitory bunk bed the next day. Everything had been moving along nicely, and my shirt and pants were off, but when I revealed my virgin status, he became (perhaps rightfully) afraid I would form an unbreakable one-way bond with him and fled. Sophomore year, I transferred to a small liberal arts school in Ohio that was known for having been the first college to admit women and African Americans, as well as for its polyamorous, bi-curious student body. I was neither, but it did seem like a good, supportive environment in which to finally get the ball rolling.

Oberlin was a free-love fantasia. During the first rainstorm of the year, nude students took to the quad, slathering one another's bodies in mud. (I wore a tankini.) People referred to each other as "former lovers, current friends." There was a student-run sex seminar where every year a boy and a girl were recruited to show their penis and vagina, respectively, to an eager crowd of aspiring Dr. Ruth Westheimers.

I really felt like the oldest virgin in town, and I probably was, save for a busty punk girl from Olympia, Washington, who was equally frustrated; she and I would often meet up in our nightgowns to discuss the lack of prospects. Just two Emily Dickinsons with facial piercings, wondering what life had in store for us and whether we had unwittingly crossed the divide between innocent and pathetic.

"Josh Krolnik ran his fingers along the elastic band of my underwear! What do we think that means?"

"He did that to me, too . . ."

We even noted, with no small amount of terror, that the guy who wore a purple bathrobe to every class had a girl in Superman-print pajamas who seemed to love him. They looked at each other gooey eyed, deep in their own (no doubt sexual) world of loungewear.

The pickings were slim, especially if, like me, you were over bisexuals. At least half the straight men on campus played Dungeons & Dragons, and another quarter eschewed footwear entirely. The cutest guy I had seen at school so far, a long-haired rock-climber named Privan, had risen from his desk at the end of class to reveal he was wearing a flowing white skirt. It was clear that I was going to have to make some concessions in order to experience carnal love.

·  ✐  ·

I met Jonah* in the cafeteria. He didn't have a specific style beyond dressing vaguely like a middle-aged lesbian. He was small but strong. (Guys under five-foot-five seemed to be my lot in life.) He wore a t-shirt from his high school spirit day (a high school with a spirit day! how quaint!), and his approach to the eternal buffet that was the cafeteria was pretty genteel, which I liked—even the vegans tended to pile their plates like the apocalypse was coming and return to their dorms catatonic from the effort of digesting. I casually mentioned how frustrated I was by my inability to get to Kentucky for a journalism project, and he immediately offered his services. Though struck by his generosity, I didn't really want to take a five-hour drive with a stranger. However, five to forty-five minutes of sex seemed okay.

The best way to do this, obviously, was to throw a wine-and-

---

* Name changed to protect the truly innocent.

cheese party, which I did, in my eight-by-ten-foot room on the "quiet floor" of East Hall. Procuring wine entailed mounting my bike and riding seven subzero miles to a package store in nearby Lorain that didn't ID, so it ended up being beer and cheese and a big box of Carr's assorted party crackers. Jonah was "casually" invited in a group email that made me sound a lot more relaxed ("Hey y'all, sometimes on a Thursday night I just need to chill. DON'T YOU?") than I actually was. And he came, and he stayed, even after all my guests had packed up and gone. That's when I knew that we would at least go to sloppy second base. We talked, at first animatedly and then in the nervous half exclamations that substitute for kissing when everyone is too shy. Finally, I told him that my dad painted huge pictures of penises for a job. When he asked if we could see them online, I grabbed him by the scruff of his neck and went for it. I removed my shirt almost immediately, as I had with the pilot, which seemed to impress him. Continuing in the key of bold, I hopped up to get the condom from the "freshman survival pack" we had been given (even though I was a sophomore, and even though I was pretty sure if the apocalypse did come we were going to need a lot more than fake Ray-Bans, a granola bar, and some mini-Band-Aids).

Meanwhile, across campus, my friend Audrey was in a private hell of her own creation. She had been in a war with her roommate all semester, a voluptuous, Ren Faire–loving Philadelphian who was the lust object of every LARPer and black-metal aficionado on campus. Audrey just wanted some quiet time to read *The New Republic* and iChat with her boyfriend in Virginia, while her roommate was now dating a kid who had tried to cook meth in the dorm kitchen, warranting an emergency visit from men in hazmat suits. Audrey asked that her roommate not keep her NuvaRing birth control in the minifridge, which the girl took as an unforgivable affront to her honor.

Before coming out to my beer-and-cheese soiree, Audrey had left her roommate a note: "If you could please have quieter sex as we approach our midterms, I'd really appreciate it." Her roommate's response was to burn Audrey's note, scatter the ashes across the floor, and leave a note of her own: "U R a frigid bitch. Get the sand out of UR vagina."

Audrey ran back to my room, hoping for a sleepover. She was sobbing, terrified that the burnt note was just a precursor to serious bodily harm, and also pretty sure I was alone, finishing the cheese, so she flung my door open without knocking—only to find Jonah on top of me. She immediately understood the magnitude of the occasion and, through her tears, cried, "Mazel tov!"

I didn't tell Jonah I was a virgin, just that I hadn't done it "that much." I was sure I had already broken my hymen in high school while crawling over a fence in Brooklyn in pursuit of a cat that didn't want to be rescued. Still, it hurt more than I'd expected and in a different way, too—duller, less like a stab wound and more like a headache. He was nervous, and, in a nod to gender equality, neither of us came. Afterward we lay there and talked, and I could tell he was a good person, whatever that even means.

·  ❦  ·

I awoke the next morning, just like I did every morning, and proceeded to do all my normal things: I called my mother, drank three cups of orange juice, ate half a block of the sharp cheddar that had been sitting out since the night before, and listened to girl-with-guitar music. I looked at pictures of cute things on the Internet and inspected my bikini line for exciting ingrown hairs. I checked my email, folded my sweaters, then unfolded all the sweaters in the process of trying to decide which sweater to wear. That night, lying down felt the same, and sleep came easily. No floodgate had been opened. No vault of true womanhood unlocked. She remained, and she was me.

Jonah and I only had sex once. The next day, he stopped by to say that he thought we'd done it too soon, and we should take a few weeks to get to know each other better. Then he asked me to be his girlfriend, put on my hot-pink bicycle helmet, and proclaimed it was "the going-steady helmet," giving me a manic thumbs-up. I "dated" him for twelve hours, then ended it in the laundry room of his dormitory. Over Christmas break, he sent me a Facebook message that read, simply: "Your Hot."

Sex was clearly easier to have than I had given it credit for. It occurred to me that I had, for the past few years, set my sights on boys who weren't interested in me, and this was because *I* wasn't ready. Despite all the movies about wayward prep-school girls I liked to watch, my high school years had been devoted to loving my pets, writing poems about back-alley love, and surrendering my body only to my own fantasies. And I wasn't ready to let go of that yet. I was sure that, once I let someone penetrate me, my world would change in some indescribable yet fundamental way. I would never be able to hug my parents with the same innocence, and being alone with myself would have a different tenor. How could I ever experience true solitude again when I'd had someone poking around my insides?

How permanent virginity feels, and then how inconsequential. After Jonah, I could barely remember the sensation of lack, the embarrassment, and the feelings of urgency. I remember passing the punk girl arm in arm with her boyfriend senior year, and we didn't even exchange a survivor's nod. She was likely having sex every night, her ample bosom heaving in time to some hard-core music, our bond erased by experience. We weren't part of any club anymore, just part of the world. Good for her.

Only later did sex and identity become one. I wrote that virginity-loss scene almost word for word in my first film, *Creative Nonfiction,* minus the part where Audrey busted down the door, afraid for her life. When I performed that sex scene, my first, I felt more changed than I had by the actual experience of having sex with Jonah. Like that was just sex, but this was my work.

# *Platonic Bed Sharing*
*A Great Idea (for People Who Hate Themselves)*

FOR A LONG TIME, I wasn't sure if I liked sex. I liked everything that led up to it: the guessing, the tentative, loaded interactions, the stilted conversation on the cold walks home, looking at myself in the mirror in someone else's closet-sized bathroom. I liked the glimpse it gave me into my partner's subconscious, which was maybe the only time I actually believed anyone besides me even existed. I liked the part where I got the sense that someone else could, maybe even did, desire me. But sex itself was a mystery. Nothing quite fit. Intercourse felt, often, like shoving a loofah into a Mason jar. And I could never sleep afterward. If we parted ways, my mind was buzzing and I couldn't get clean. If we slept in the same bed, my legs cramped and I stared at the wall. How could I sleep when the person beside me had firsthand knowledge of my mucous membranes?

Junior year of college, I found a solution to this problem: platonic bed sharing, the act of welcoming a person you're attracted to into your bed for a night that contains everything but sex. You will laugh. You will cuddle. You will avoid all the humiliations and unwanted noises that accompany amateur sex.

Sharing beds platonically offered me the chance to show off my nightclothes like a 1950s housewife and experience a frisson of passion, minus the invasion of my insides. It was efficient, like what pioneers do to stay warm on icy mountain passes. The only question was to spoon or not to spoon. The next day I felt the warmth of having been wanted, minus the terrible flashes of dick, balls, and spit that played on a loop the day after a real sexual encounter.

Of course at the time I was doing it, I had none of this self-awareness about my own motives and considered platonic bed sharing my lot: not ugly enough to be repulsive and not beautiful enough to seal the deal. My bed was a rest stop for the lonely, and I was the spinster innkeeper.

·  🐚  ·

I shared a bed with my sister, Grace, until I was seventeen years old. She was afraid to sleep alone and would begin asking me around 5:00 P.M. every day whether she could sleep with me. I put on a big show of saying no, taking pleasure in watching her beg and sulk, but eventually I always relented. Her sticky, muscly little body thrashed beside me every night as I read Anne Sexton, watched reruns of *SNL*, sometimes even as I slipped my hand into my underwear to figure some

stuff out. Grace had the comforting, sleep-inducing proper-
ties of a hot-water bottle or a cat.

I always pretended to hate it. I complained to my parents:
"No other teenagers have to share beds unless they're
REALLY POOR! Someone please get her to sleep alone!
She's ruining my life!" After all, she had her own bed that
she *chose* not to sleep in. "Take it up with her," they said, well
aware that I, too, got something out of the arrangement.

The truth is I had no right to complain, having been af-
fected by childhood "sleep issues" so severe that my father
says he didn't experience an uninterrupted night's rest between 1986 and 1998. To me, sleep equaled death. How was
closing your eyes and losing consciousness any different from
death? What separated temporary loss of consciousness from
permanent obliteration? I could not face this prospect by myself, so every night I'd have to be dragged kicking and screaming to my room, where I demanded a series of tuck-in rituals
so elaborate that I'm shocked my parents never hit me (hard).

Then around 1:00 A.M., once my parents were finally
asleep, I would creep into their room and kick my father out
of bed, settling into the warmth of his spot and passing out
beside my mother, the brief guilt of displacing him far out-
weighed by the joy of no longer being alone. It only occurred
to me recently that this was probably my way of making sure
my parents didn't ever have sex again.

My poor father, desperate to end the cold war that had
broken out around sleep in our house, told me that if I retired at nine every night and stayed peacefully in my room he
would wake me at 3:00 A.M. and carry me into his own. This
seemed reasonable: I wouldn't have the opportunity to be
dead for too many hours by myself, and he would stop yelling
at me quite so much. He kept his end up, dutifully rising at
3:00 A.M. to come and move me.

Then one night, when I was eleven, he didn't. I didn't notice, until I awoke at 7:00 A.M. to the sounds of our morning, Grace already downstairs enjoying organic frozen waffles and Cartoon Network. I looked around groggily, outraged by the light streaming in through my window.

"YOU BROKE YOUR PROMISE," I sobbed.

"But you were okay," he pointed out. I couldn't argue. He was right. It was a relief not to have seen the world at 3:00 A.M.

As soon as my issues disappeared, Grace's replaced them, as if sleep disorders were a family business being passed down through the ages. And though I persisted in complaining, I still secretly cherished her presence in my bed. The light snoring, the way she put herself to sleep by counting cracks in the ceiling, noting them with a mousy sound that is best spelled like this: *Miep Miep Miep.* The way her little pajama top rode up over her belly. My baby girl. I was keeping her safe until morning.

It all began with Jared Krauter. He was the first thing I noticed at the New School orientation, leaning against the wall talking to a girl with a buzz cut—his anime eyes, his flared women's jeans, his thick helmet of Prince Valiant hair. He was the first guy I'd seen in Keds, and I was moved by the confidence it took for him to wear delicate lady shoes. I was moved by his entire being. If I'd been alone, I would have slid down the back of a door and sighed like Natalie Wood in *Splendor in the Grass.*

This was not technically the first time I'd seen Jared. He was a city kid, and he used to hang around outside my high school waiting for his friend from camp. Every time I spotted him I'd think to myself, That is one hot piece of ass.

"Hey," I said, sidling up to him in my flesh-toned tube top. "I think I've seen you outside Saint Ann's. You know Steph, right?"

Jared was friendlier than cool guys are supposed to be. He invited me to come see his band play later that night. It was the first of many gigs I'd attend—and the first of many nights we'd spend in my top bunk, pressed against each other like sardines, never kissing. At first, it seemed like shyness. Like he was a gentleman and we were taking our time. Surely it would happen at some point, and we'd remember these tentative days with a laugh, then fuck passionately. But days stretched into weeks stretched into months, and his fondness for me never took a turn for the sexual. I pined for him, despite sleeping pressed against his body. His skin smelled like soap and subway, and when he slept, his eyelids fluttered.

Despite his indie-rock swagger and access to free alcohol via his job as a bouncer, Jared was a virgin just like me. We found the same things funny (a Mexican girl in our dorm who told us her parents live in "a condom in Florida"), the same food delicious (onion rings, perhaps the reason we never kissed), and the same music heady (whatever he said I should listen to). He was a shield against loneliness, against fights with my mom and C-minus papers and mean bartenders who didn't buy my fake ID. When I told him I was transferring schools, he teared up. The next week, he dropped out.

At Oberlin, I missed Jared. His midsection against my back. The slightly sour smell of his breath when it caught my cheek. Coagreeing to sleep through the alarm. But it didn't take me long to replace him.

First came Dev Coughlin, a piano student I noticed on his way back from the shower and became determined to kiss. He had the severe face and impossibly great hair of Alain

Delon but said "wicked" more than most French New Wave actors. One night we walked out to the softball field, where I told him I was a virgin, and he told me he had mold in his dorm room and needed a place to crash. What followed was an intense two-week period of bed sharing, not totally platonic because we kissed twice. The rest of the time I writhed around like a cat in heat, hoping he'd graze me in a way I could translate into pleasure. I'm not sure if the mold was eradicated or my desperation became too much for him, but he moved back to his room in mid-October. I mourned the loss for a few weeks before switching over to Jerry Barrow.

Jerry was a physics major from Baltimore who wore glasses, and unusually short pants (shants), and who alternated between the screen names Sherylcrowsingsmystory and Boobynation. If Jared and Dev had been beautiful to me, then Jerry was pure utility. I knew we would never fall in love, but his solid physical presence soothed me, and we fell into a week of bed sharing. He had enough self-respect to remove himself from the situation after I invited his best friend, Josh Berenson, to sleep on the other side of me.

Right on, bro.

Josh was the genre of guy I like to call "hot for camp," and he had a nihilistic, cartoonish sense of humor that I enjoyed. Despite my practicing "the push in," the move where you advance your ass slowly but surely onto the crotch of an unsuspecting man, he showed no interest in engaging physically with me. The closest we came was when he ran a flattened palm over my left breast, like he was an alien who had been given a lesson in human sexuality by a robot.

By this point, word was getting around: Lena likes to share beds.

Guy friends who came over to study would just assume they were staying. Boys who lived across campus would ask to crash so that they could get to class early in the morning. My reputation was preceding me, and not in the way I had always dreamed of. (Example: *Have you met Lena? I have never met a more simultaneously creative and sexual woman. Her hips are so flexible she could join the circus, but she's too smart.*) But I had standards, and I wouldn't share a bed with just anyone. Among the army I refused:

Nikolai, a Russian guy in pointy black boots who read to me from a William Burroughs book about cats, his face very close to mine. He was a twenty-six-year-old sophomore who referred to vaginas as "pink" like it was 1973.

Jason, a psych major who told me his dream was to have seven children he could take to Yankees games with him so they could wear letterman jackets that collectively spelled out the team name.

Patrick, so sweet and small that I did let him into my bed, just once, and in the wee hours I awoke to find his arm hovering above me, as if he were too afraid to let it rest on my side. "The Hover-Spooner" we called him forevermore, even after he became known around campus as the guy who poured vodka up his butt through a funnel.

I learned to masturbate the summer after third grade. I read about it in a puberty book, which described it as "touching your private parts until you have a very good feeling, like a sneeze." The idea of a vaginal sneeze seemed embarrassing at best and disgusting at worst, but it was a pretty boring summer, so I decided to explore my options.

I approached it clinically over a number of days, lying on the bath mat in the only bathroom in our summer house that had a locking door. I touched myself using different pressures, rhythms. The sensation was pleasant in the same way as a foot rub. One afternoon, lying there on the mat, I looked up to find myself eye to eye with a baby bat who was hanging upside down on the curtain rod. We stared at each other in stunned silence.

Finally one day, toward the end of the summer, the hard work paid off, and I felt the sneeze, which was actually more like a seizure. I took a moment on the bath mat to collect myself, then rose to wash my hands. I checked to make sure my face wasn't frozen into any strange position, that I still looked like my parents' child, before I headed downstairs.

Sometimes as an adult, when I'm having sex, images from the bathroom come to me unbidden. The knotty-pine paneling of the ceiling, eaten away like Swiss cheese. My mother's fancy soaps in a caddy above the claw-foot tub. The rusty bucket where we keep our toilet paper. I can smell the wood. I can hear boats revving on the lake, my sister dragging her tricycle back and forth on the porch. I am hot. I am hungry for a snack. But mostly, I am alone.

When I graduated and moved back in with my parents, the bed sharing continued—Bo, Kevin, Norris—and became a real point of contention. My mother expressed distress, not only at having strange men in her house but at the fact that I had an interest in such a thankless activity. "It's worse than fucking them all!" she said.

"You don't owe everybody a *crash pad*," my father said.

They didn't get it. They didn't get any of it. Hadn't they ever felt alone before?

I remembered seventh grade, when my friend Natalie and I started sleeping in her TV room on Friday and Saturday nights, every weekend. We would watch Comedy Central or *Saturday Night Live* and eat cold pizza until one or two, pass out on the foldout couch, then awake at dawn to see her older sister Holly and her albino boyfriend sneaking into her bedroom. This went on for a few months, reliable and bliss-ful and oddly domestic, our routine as set as any eighty-year-old couple's. But one Friday after school she coolly told me she "needed space" (where a twelve-year-old girl got this line I will never know), and I was devastated. Back at home, my own room felt like a prison. I had gone from perfect com-panionship to none at all.

In response I wrote a short story, tragic and Carver-esque, about a young woman who had come to the city to make it as a Broadway actress and been seduced by a controlling con-struction worker who had forced her into domestic slavery. She spent her days washing dishes and frying eggs and fight-ing with the slumlord of their tenement apartment. The con-clusion of the story involved her creeping to a phone booth to call her mother in Kansas City, a place I had never been. Her mother announced she had disowned her, so she kept walking, toward who knows what. I don't remember any spe-cific phrasing except this closing sentence: *She wanted to sleep without the pressure of his arms.*

·   ·

For a brief time I was in a relationship with a former televi-sion personality who, steeped in the tragedy of early failure, had moved to Los Angeles to make a new life for himself. I was living at a residential hotel in LA, in a beige room that overlooked the garden of two elderly male nudists, and I was lonely as hell and didn't hate kissing him. He still vaguely resembled a person I had seen on my TV as a tween, and when we went out together, I often watched the faces of wait-resses and cabdrivers, looking for a flash of recognition. But kissing was as far as it ever went. He was, he told me, scarred emotionally by a former relationship, a dead dog, and some-thing related to the Iraq War (which he had not, to my knowl-edge, fought in). I liked his apartment. He had blown-glass lamps, a graying black lab, a refrigerator full of Perrier. He kept his home office neat, a chalkboard with his ideas scrawled on it the only decoration. Driving through a rain-storm one night we hydroplaned, and he grabbed my leg like a dad would. We took a hike in Malibu and shared ice cream. I stayed with him while he had walking pneumonia, heating soup and pouring him glass after glass of ginger ale and feel-ing his fevered forehead as he slept. He warned me of the life that was coming for me if I wasn't careful. Success was a scary thing for a young person, he said. I was twenty-four and he was thirty-three ("Jesus's age," he reminded me more than a few times). There was something tender about him, broken and gentle, and I could imagine that sex with him might be similar. I wouldn't have to pretend like I did with other guys. Maybe we would both cry. Maybe it would feel just as good as sharing a bed.

On Valentine's Day, I put on lace underwear and begged him to please, finally, have sex with me. The litany of excuses he presented in response was comic in its tragedy: "I want to get to know you." "I don't have a condom." "I'm scared, be-cause I just like you too much." He took an Ambien and fell asleep, arm over my side, and as I lay there, wide awake and itchy in my lingerie set, it occurred to me: this was humiliat-ing, unsexy, and, worst sin of all, boring. This wasn't comfort. This was paralysis. This was distance passing for connection. I was being desexualized in slow motion, becoming a teddy bear with breasts.

I was a working woman. I deserved kisses. I deserved to be treated like a piece of meat but also respected for my intellect. And I could afford a cab home. So I called one, and his sad dog with the Hebrew name watched me hop his fence and pace at the curbside until my taxi came.

Here's who it's okay to share a bed with:

Your sister if you're a girl, your brother if you're a boy, your mom if you're a girl, and your dad if you're under twelve or he's over ninety. Your best friend. A carpenter you picked up at the key-lime-pie stand in Red Hook. A bellhop you met in the business center of a hotel in Colorado. A Spanish model, a puppy, a kitten, one of those domesticated minigoats. A heating pad. An empty bag of pita chips. The love of your life.

Here's who it's not okay to share a bed with:

Anyone who makes you feel like you're invading their space. Anyone who tells you that they "just can't be alone right now." Anyone who doesn't make you feel like sharing a bed is the coziest and most sensual activity they could possibly be undertaking (unless, of course, it is one of the aforementioned relatives; in that case, they should act lovingly but also reserved/slightly annoyed).

Now, look over at the person beside you. Do they meet these criteria? If not, remove them or remove yourself. You're better off alone.

# 18 Unlikely Things
# I've Said Flirtatiously

**1.** "My nickname in high school was Blow-Job Lena, but because I gave NO blow jobs! Like when you call a fat guy Skinny Joe."

**2.** "I only get BO in one armpit. Swear. Same with my mother."

**3.** "I once woke up in the middle of sex with a virtual stranger!"

**4.** "Let's meet for coffee, yeah. Well, not *coffee* coffee. Like a different drink, because coffee gave me a colon infection and I had to wear this paper underwear the hospital gave me."

**5.** "Not to sound like a total hippie, but I cured my HPV with acupuncture."

**6.** "He had no legs, and HE wasn't into ME. But that's not why we stopped being friends."

**7.** "I've never seen *Star Wars* OR *The Godfather,* so that would be a good excuse for us to spend a bunch of time together."

**8.** "I was a really chubby teenager, covered in a thick layer of grease. Seriously, I'll show you a picture."

**9.** "You should come over. My dad is super funny."

**10.** "I'm the kind of person who should probably date older guys, but I can't deal with their balls."

**11.** "I'm obsessed with the curtains in your van!"

**12.** "Come to my party! We can't talk or make noise because my neighbor is dying, but I spent a ton of money on salami."

**13.** "Get closer to my belly button. Does this look like shingles, scabies, both, or neither?"

**14.** "This one time, I thought I was petting my hairless cat, and it was actually my mom's vagina. Over the covers, of course!"

**15.** "Sorry if my breath is kind of metallic. It's my medication. Weird fact: I'm on the highest dose of this stuff on record."

**16.** "I seriously don't care if you shoplift."

**17.** "I appreciate that you didn't point out my huge weight loss. It's exhausting, everyone being like 'How did you do it? Blah-blah-blah.'"

**18.** "My sister went back inside, so I think we're safe. Wanna sit on the rock that doesn't have algae? Or the algae one is fine, too."

# *Igor*

*Or, My Internet Boyfriend Died and So Can Yours*

THE COMPUTERS just show up one day. We come in from recess, and there they are, seven gray boxes on a long table in the fifth-floor hallway.

"We got computers!" our teacher announces. "And they are going to help us learn!"

Everyone is buzzing, but I am immediately suspicious. What is so great about our hall being full of ugly squat robots? Why is everyone cheering like idiots? What can we learn from these machines that we can't from our teachers?

The boys especially are transfixed, spending every free moment tap-tap-tapping on the keyboards, playing a simplistic game that involves stacking blocks in an effort to make them explode. I stay away. I have only touched one other computer, at my friend Marissa's house, and found the experience disconcerting. There was something sinister about the green letters and numbers that flashed on the screen as the computer booted up, and I hated the way Marissa stopped answering questions or noticing me the second it was turned on.

My distaste for computers has an almost-political fervor: they're changing our society, I say, and for the worse. Let's act human. Converse. Use our handwriting. I ask to be excused from typing class, where we use a program called Mavis Beacon Teaches Typing to learn which finger should touch which letter. (Pinkie on *P*, she says. Pinkie on *P*.) While the others try to please Mavis, I write in my notebook.

At parent-teacher conferences my teacher tells my mother and father that I show "a real hostility toward technology." She wishes I was willing to "embrace new developments in the classroom." When my mother announces we will be getting one of our own at home, I go to my room and turn on the tiny black-and-white TV I bought at a yard sale, refusing to come out for over an hour.

It arrives one evening after school, an Apple with a monitor the size of a moving box. A guy with a ponytail installs it, shows my mother how to use the CD-ROM drive, and asks if I want to see the "preinstalled" games. I shake my head: *No. No, I don't.*

But the computer exerts a magnetic pull, sitting there in the middle of our living room, humming ever so slightly. I watch as my babysitter walks my sister through a game of Oregon Trail, only to have her entire digital family die of dysentery before they can ford the river. My mother types a Word document with her two pointer fingers. "Don't you want to try it?" she asks.

Finally, the temptation is too great. I want to try, to see what all the fuss is about, but I don't want to be a hypocrite. I already went back on being a vegetarian and was so ashamed

I told the girls at lunch that my sandwich was tofu prosciutto. I have to be true to myself. I can't keep rejiggering my identity, and hating computers is a part of my identity. One day my mother is in her bedroom organizing her shoes, and the coast is clear. I walk into the living room, sit down in the cold metal office chair, and slowly extend my finger toward the power button. Listen to it boot up, ping, and purr. I feel an exhilarating sense of trespass.

In fifth grade we all get screen names. We message with one another, but we also go to chat rooms, digital hangouts with names like Teen Hang and A Place for Friends. It takes me a little while to wrap my head around the idea of anonymity. Of people I can't see who can't see me. Of being seen without being seen at all. Katie Pomerantz and I jointly take on the persona of a fourteen-year-old model named Mariah, who has flowing black hair, B-cup breasts, and an endless supply of smiley faces. Aware of Mariah's incredible power, we ensnare boys, promising them we are beautiful, popular, and looking for love, as well as rich off of our teen-model earnings. We giggle as we take turns typing, reveling in our power. At one point, we ask a boy in Delaware to check the tag of his jeans and tell us the brand.

"They're Wrangler," he writes back. "My mom got them at Walmart."

Feverish with triumph, we log out.

Juliana is new to ninth grade. She doesn't know anyone, but she has the confidence of someone who has been popular since kindergarten. She's a punk: her nose is pierced, and her hair is spiked. She wears a homemade T-shirt that reads LEFTOVER CRACK, and her face is so beautiful that sometimes I can't help but imagine it superimposed over my own. Juliana is a vegan for political reasons and seems to genuinely enjoy music without a melody. When she tells me that she's had sex—in an alleyway, no less, with a twenty-year-old guy—it takes me a week to recover.

"I was wearing a skirt, so he just pulled my underwear to the side," she says, as casually as if she were telling me what her mom made for dinner.

Two months into school she uses her fake ID to get a tattoo, a nautical star on the back of her neck, the lines thick and inelegant.

I ask to run my fingers over the scab, unable to believe this will exist *forever.*

A lot of Juliana's punk friends live in New Jersey, where she often goes on the weekends for "shows." At lunch, we look at their homemade Angelfire.com websites, one of which has an image of a decomposing baby carcass on the home page. But mostly they post pictures of themselves sweaty and piled high in front of makeshift stages. It's hard to tell who's in the band and who is just hanging out. She points out Shane, a pretty blond she has a crush on. His website is called Str8Outta-Compton, a reference I won't get for another ten years. In one of Shane's photos, a picture of a concert in a cramped basement, I notice a boy, tan with chubby cheeks and vacant blue eyes, moshing off to the side, a bandanna tied around his head. "Who's that?" I ask.

"His name is Igor," Juliana tells me. "He's Russian. Vegan, too. He's really nice."

"He's cute," I say.

That night, an instant-message bubble pops up from Pyro0001. I accept.

**Pyro0001:** Hey, it's Igor.

For the next three months, Igor and I instant message for hours every night. I get home around three thirty, and he comes home at four, so I make myself a snack and wait for his name to appear. I want to let him say "hey" first, but usually I can't wait that long. We talk about animals. About school. About the injustices of the world, most of them directed at innocent animals who can't defend themselves against the evils of humanity. He's a man of few words, but the words he uses are perfect to me.

I am no longer opposed to the computer. I am in love with it.

No guys like me at school. Some ignore me while others are outright cruel, but none want to kiss me. I'm still distraught over a seventh-grade breakup and refuse to attend parties I know my ex will be at. At this point, my heartbreak has lasted twenty-four times as long as our relationship.

Igor wants to see a photo of me, so I send him one of me against my bedroom wall, on which I have drawn trees and nudes with a Sharpie. My hair hangs in a yellow, flat-ironed curtain, and I am cracking a glossy half smile. Igor says I look like Christina Aguilera. He's a punk, so it seems more like a factual assessment than a compliment, but I am thrilled.

We message through dinner, through fights with our parents. He describes how quiet it is when he gets home, how his parents aren't back until eight. He says "brb" when he goes to the door to get his delivery dinner, which is usually eggplant parm minus the parm. He tells me that he goes to the kind of school that has popular kids and losers, jocks, and freaks. A big public school with a class full of strangers. My school is supposed to be different, small and creative and inclusive, but sometimes I feel just as isolated as he does. I start describing kids at school as "bimbos" and "fakes," words I never would have thought to use before he introduced them. Words he'll understand and that will draw him to me.

When I go on vacation with my family, I ask the hotel office to let me use the computer so I can send Igor an email on Valentine's Day. He tells me he doesn't want to send me a new picture of himself because he's had "some pimples" lately. My father is irritated that I take the time away from the beach to sit in a windowless office with a woman smoking Newports and send love notes to someone I've never met. He doesn't get it. He doesn't even have email.

Juliana says that Igor's friend Shane says that Igor says he really likes me. This emboldens me to ask him to talk on the phone. He seems eager and takes my number but never calls. Juliana says she thinks he may be self-conscious about his accent.

**Trixiebelle86:** If u don't like the fone may-b we cud meet in person?

He agrees to meet me the following Saturday on Saint Mark's Place. He'll take the train in, and we'll find each other on the corner. I go, in a tank top, cargo pants, and a shrunken denim jacket, even though it's freezing. I'm so nervous, I arrive twenty minutes early. He isn't there yet. I wait another half hour, but he never comes. I try and look relaxed as pierced NYU kids and pink-haired Asian girls stream past me. I go home and log on, but he isn't there either.

The next day, he messages me:

**Pyro0001:** Sorry. Grounded. May-B sum other time.

Gradually, Igor stops messaging me. When he does make contact, it's only to respond. He never initiates. Every time that ping sounds, signaling a message, I run to the computer, hoping it's him. But it's only John, a kid from a nearby school who excels at break dancing, or my friend Stephanie, complaining about her Peruvian father's strict rules about skirt length. Igor doesn't ask me any questions anymore. Our relationship had hummed with possibility: the possibility of meeting, of liking each other even more in person than we did online, of falling in love with each other's eyes and smell and sneakers. Now it's over before it began. I wonder whether I can consider him an ex.

One day, in late summer, Juliana IMs me.

**Northernstar2001:** Lena Igor is dead.
**Trixiebelle86:** What???
**Northernstar2001:** Shane IMd me. He had a methadone overdose, choked on his own tongue in his basement. Its fukked. He's an only child and his parents don't like speak English.
**Trixiebelle86:** Did Shane say if Igor stopped liking me?

I'm not sure who to tell because I'm not sure who will care, and I don't want to explain the whole thing to anyone. It was impossible for my parents to understand the reality of Igor when he was alive, so why would they get it when he was dead?

A year later I have to change my screen name because a boy at school, a massive hairy boy with a face like a Picasso painting, sends me an email saying he's going to rape me and cover me in barbecue sauce. He's the only guy who likes me in that way, but I wish he wouldn't. He mentions having a machete and attaches a photograph of a kitten that has been stuffed inside a bottle and left to die. My father is justifiably angry and calls my uncle, who is a lawyer and says the police need to be involved. For the first and last time, I am escorted home from school by the cops. When they go to his house, they find he has printed and saved all of our instant messages, pages and pages of them. One of the officers implies I shouldn't have been so nice to him if I didn't like him "that way." I tell them I just felt sorry for him. They say I should be more careful in the future. I am ashamed.

My new screen name includes my real name and is only shared with select friends and family, but I transfer all my contacts, so I can always see who is logged on when. One day, in my HERE TO CHAT bar, I see him: Pyro0001. The world goes fast, then slow again, the way it does sometimes when I get up to pee in the night and the whole house sounds like it's saying *Lena, Lena, Lena.*

"Hey," I type.

The name disappears.

I walk around for the rest of that day like I've seen a ghost. I type his full name into multiple search engines, looking for an obituary or some evidence that he existed. I mean, Juliana knew him. She met him. She heard his accent. He was real.

He is dead. Fake people don't die. Fake people don't even exist.

Years later, I will give his last name to a character on my television show. A smoke signal, so that whoever wants to know can know: he was kind to me. He had things to say. There was a way in which I loved him. I did, I did, I did.

## *Sharing Concerns*
### *My Worst Email Ever, with Footnotes*

---

September 27, 2010

A.,[*]

Before I get back to writing I had to jot this down to you.[†]
Like, the last six times we've spoken it has ended with a
series of long silences where I say something, then an-

[*] Addressing my beloved by a single initial seemed romantic, like the desperate
and secretive correspondence of two married intellectuals in the late nineteenth
century. Lest the meddling postmaster discover our identities and reveal our affair
to our vindictive spouses, we will communicate using a code. That code shall be: the
first letter of our names.

[†] "Jot" is a pretty casual word for the dissertation on emotional dysfunction that
follows. Throughout the course of this relationship, I wrote A. epics that he would
answer with either a single word ("cool," "sure") or a screed on a totally unrelated
matter that was currently nagging him, like the impossibility of finding fashionable
winter boots or the lack of modern-day Hemingways. I would comb these emails,
searching desperately for a hint that they were truly for and about me, and come
away knowing only that they had, in fact, been sent to my address.

other thing to modify it, then I sort of apologize, then I sort of unapologize.* That would be funny as a scene in an indie rom-com,† funny the first few times it happens, but it doesn't need to happen because I should just be able to get off the phone and say "enjoy your day, A., I'll talk with you soon." I'm obviously fishing for stuff and then explaining it away between silences.

I should stop apologizing for being overly analytical about this, even though I am sorry (not to you but in a deeper way, sorry for my brain chemistry and who I am. I do what I can that isn't heroin to modify it but I was born as anxious and obsessive as any incredibly gorgeous child ever could be.)‡ The dynamics of romantic relationships are obviously fascinating to us both, artistically and theoretically.§ Ditto sex. But it's harder to incor-

---

* Me: So . . .

[*Beat.*]

Me: Are you still there? I'm feeling kind of . . . I just wonder if perhaps when I say something you could say something because that is called . . .

[*Beat.*]

Me: A conversation.

† Ironic references to rom-coms are a great way to show that you are NOT the kind of girl/woman who cares about romantic conventions. A. and I often disagreed about what to watch. His interests lay mostly with masculine classics from the 1980s, while I tended (and still tend) to want to watch films with female protagonists. Rather than admit that he didn't want to waste two hours watching a woman's interior life unfold, he would tell me these films "lack structure." Structure was a constant topic. He built shelves, wrote scripts, and dressed for the cold weather with a rigor and discipline that, while initially intriguing, came to feel like living under a Communist regime. Rules, rules, rules: no mixing navy and black, no stacking books horizontally, pour your beverage into a twenty-ounce Mason jar, and make sure something big happens on page 10.

‡ This is a reference to when I told him that, as a child, I was hypnotized by my own beauty. This was the time in life before I learned it wasn't considered appropriate by society at large to like yourself.

§ Although he worked a job that involved heavy lifting and hard labor, his true passion was writing fiction, and after much cajoling on my part he gave me one of his stories to read. It was the twenty-page account of a young man very much like himself trying, and failing, to seduce an Asian girl who worked at J.Crew in Soho. Although the prose was unusual and funny, the story sat with me like a bad meal. It

porate into your actual working life in a way that's comfortable.*

I obviously like you a lot. Not in a scary oppressive way[†] and not in an "I just came looking at a picture of you" way (though I did do that)[‡] but in the way that I am going out of my way to make you a part of my life, or just to figure out what it could be. I was so ready to spend four months in Los Angeles really embracing this alien city of bad trees, letting my parents visit me and hiking and maybe dating some douche bag just for the story.[§] A week before I met you I quipped to someone "I would be a horrible girlfriend at this point in my life, because I'm both needy and unavailable."[¶] Jokes aren't just jokes.[**]

took me about twenty-four hours to realize the issue: that I could feel, in nearly every sentence, an essential disdain for womankind that was neither examined nor explained. It was the same feeling I had experienced after my initial read of Philip Roth's *Goodbye, Columbus* in eighth grade: I love this book, but I don't want to meet this man. But, in this case, it was: This story is okay and its author has already come in me.

* The first week we met, I slept at his house every night. Time stopped in his bedroom, which was windowless and overly warm. Each day we took a new step together: flossed our teeth, shared a bagel, fell asleep without having sex. He admitted to having an upset stomach. By the time I emerged from his home on Friday morning, we had essentially performed the first year of a relationship in five days. I got on the plane to Los Angeles, unsure of when we'd see each other again. I was pretty sure I'd seen him cry a little bit when he dropped me at the subway.

† Perhaps, yes, in that way.

‡ As an experiment. It was similar to looking at an empty vase or staring out a window.

§ On this trip, my first as a working woman, I was renting a house in the hills above Hollywood. It had been pitched to me as "chic" and "within walking distance of chic things" but was small and damp, windowless on three sides, and had the boxy nondescript façade of a meth lab. Sandwiched between the homes of a failed TV writer with a set of pit bulls and a queer-theory professor who wore a bolo tie and collected Murano glass, I decided that the amount of fear I felt alone in this house was directly proportional to all I would learn from living there. And so I stayed, for five months, calling it growth. One night I put on a nightgown, stepped onto the porch, looked up at the moon, and said, "Who am I?"

¶ I remember being so impressed with this turn of phrase that I carefully clocked who I had already shared it with and who I could still try it out on.

** Paraphrasing Freud.

It feels really good to check in with you, and I'm intrigued by the possibility of sharing certain kinds of concerns regularly.[*] Because I'm here and you're there it can't happen totally organically, and because I'm me I have a hard time sitting with that. So that's why I try to understand if I'll see you when I come home, or if you think about me when you jerk off,[†] or just how available you are to have your life futzed with a little bit.

The night of the party when we met, when you told me to meet you on the corner, I was really sure that I would go out there and you'd have tricked me and gone someplace else. And then you weren't exactly where you said you'd be but you were nearby.[‡]

OK,[§]

L[1]

---

[*] I wanted a boyfriend. Any boyfriend. This boyfriend, this angry little Steve McQueen face, fit my self-image nicely, but let's face it, he was in the right place at the right time. About a month into the relationship, it started to dawn on me that spending time with him gave me an empty, fluish feeling, that he hated all my song choices, and sometimes I was so bored that I started arguments just to experience the rush of almost losing him. I spent an entire three-hour car ride crying behind my sunglasses like my thirty-year marriage was ending. "I don't know what else I can try," I wept. "I can't do this anymore." "Can't or won't," he hollered like Stanley Kowalski, backing angrily into his least favorite parking spot and jerking the gear into park. Upstairs I paced, cried; he cried, too; and when I told him we could try again, he turned on his PlayStation, content.

[†] At one point I asked him this, and he responded with a trademark silence. I attempted to engage in a "sext" session, starting off with "I want to fuck you above the covers." This seemed like something Anaïs Nin might request. *No,* she would say. *Leave the covers off.* He responded with texts that read "I want to fuck you with the air conditioner on" and "I want to fuck you after I set my alarm clock for 8:45 A.M." I closed my eyes and tried to inhabit the full sensuality of his words: the cool recycled air on my neck, the knowledge that the alarm would sound just a bit before nine. It took about eleven of these texts for me to realize he was doing some kind of Dadaist performance art at my expense.

[‡] I desperately wanted this to be a metaphor for the ways love stretches us, changes us, but never betrays us.

[§] See? I'm just a chill girl writing a chill-ass email, bro.

[¶] At Christmas we had to end it for real this time. After all, he said he was incapable of love and only seeking satisfaction. I, on the other hand, was passionate and

p.s. If you don't have anything to say back to this email it will be some kind of incredible poetic justice.* Also, sorry this email is so unfunny.†

———

fully alive, electricity in every limb, a tree growing in Brooklyn. I headed to his apartment the moment he returned from his parents' house, determined to make it easy, to cut the cord on his home turf. His landlord, Kathy, tended to sit on the front stoop. An elderly woman with a mighty tattoo of a panther on her wide, fatty shoulder, she and her Yorkshire terriers kept watch over the neighborhood. But tonight Kathy was absent. Instead, a shrine of candles and flowers crowded the path to the door. Upstairs, he told me that he thought one of Kathy's dogs had probably died. We called her to see if everything was okay, but Kathy's daughter answered—Kathy had slipped in the shower. It may have been her heart. They weren't sure yet. The wake was tonight. So, my soon-to-be-ex-boyfriend and I made our way across Brooklyn to the funeral home, where we paid our respects to Kathy's gray, powdered body, stiff in a red velour sweatsuit, a pack of menthols tucked into the front pocket. Later, on A.'s couch, we held hands while he wondered whether she'd felt pain and whether his rent would go up. I clutched his hand, ready: "I love you, you know." He nodded solemnly: "I know."

* Five minutes after I pressed send on this email, he called me. "Wait, what?"

"What did you think of it?" I asked. "Do you disagree with anything I said? I mean, if you do just say so."

"I stopped reading after you said the thing about jerking off."

On the morning of New Year's Day, we had sex one last time. I didn't fully emerge from sleep as he pushed himself against my backside. We were visiting my friends, adult friends, out of the city, and I could hear their children, awake since 6:00 A.M., sliding in socks on the hardwood floor and asking for things. I want children, I thought, as he fucked me silently. My own children, someday. Then: I wonder if people fucked near me when *I* was a child. I shuddered at the thought. Before we could get back on the road, another guest rear-ended his car, and the fender fell off. Back in the city, I kissed him goodbye, then texted him a few minutes later "don't come over later, or ever." We do what we can.

† I would argue this email *is* funny, just not in the manner it was intended.

# *Girls & Jerks*

*There is a common superstition that "self-respect" is a kind of charm against snakes, something that keeps those who have it locked in some unblighted Eden, out of strange beds, ambivalent conversations, and trouble in general. It does not at all. It has nothing to do with the face of things, but concerns instead a separate peace, a private reconciliation.*

**—JOAN DIDION, "On Self-Respect"***

*I always run into strong women who are looking for weak men to dominate them.*

**—ANDY WARHOL**

* I think Joan and I are talking about slightly different sorts of self-respect. She's referring to a general sense of accountability for one's actions and a feeling that you're being truthful with yourself when you lay your head down at night. I'm more talking about sex. But also what she said.

I'VE ALWAYS BEEN ATTRACTED to jerks. They range from sassy weirdos who are ultimately pretty good guys to sociopathic sex addicts, but the common denominator is a bad attitude upon first meeting and a desire to teach me a lesson.

Fellows: If you are rude to me in a health-food store? I will be intrigued by you. If you ignore me in group conversation? I'll take note of that, too. I especially like it when a guy starts out rude, explains that it's a defense mechanism, and then turns even ruder once I get to know him. As I passed the quarter-century mark of being alive and entered into a relationship with a truly kind person, all this changed. I now consider myself in jerk recovery, so being around any of the aforementioned behaviors isn't yet safe for me.

My attraction to jerks started early. I spent my preadolescent summers in a cottage by a lake, curled on a ratty couch in my mom's MIND THE GAP t-shirt, watching movies like *Now and Then* and *The Man in the Moon*. If I took anything away from these tales of young desire, it was that if a guy really liked you he would spray you with a water gun and call you nicknames like the Blob. If he shoved you off your bike and your knees bled, it probably meant he was going to kiss you by a reservoir soon enough.

My earliest memory of sexual arousal is watching Jackie Earle Haley as Kelly Leak in *Bad News Bears*. He wore a leather jacket, rode a motorcycle before the legal age, smoked, and treated his elders with a kind of disrespect I had never seen executed by any of the boys at Quaker school. Moreover, he ogled adult women like a Hefner acolyte. Later, I was drawn to images of angry attraction, *I-want-you-despite-myself* type stuff, the kind of thing that Jane Eyre and Rochester were up to. You know the way Holly Hunter looks at William Hurt in *Broadcast News,* like she hates everything he stands for? That was dreamy. Even *9½ Weeks* made some terrible kind of sense.

All of this is natural enough—who doesn't thrill at a little push-pull, a bit of athletic conversation—but I'm the first to admit I've often taken it too far.

It's common wisdom that having a good dad tends to mean you'll pick a good man, and I have pretty much the nicest dad in the world. I don't mean nice in a neutered "yes, dear" way. I mean nice in that he has always respected my essential nature and offered me an expert mix of space and support. He's a firm but benevo-lent leader. He talks to adults like they're  juvenile delinquents and to kids like they're adults. I've often tried to write a character based on him, but it's such a chal-lenge to distill his essence. I wasn't always easy, and neither was he—after all, artists like to hole themselves up in their studios for days and pitch fits about bad lighting—but the careful, reliable attention of this man has been integral to my sense of security. To this day, the truest feeling of joy I have ever known is the door opening at a friend's house to reveal my father—in his tweed overcoat—there to rescue me from a bad play date.

Once, when I was five, I was at an art opening talking to a fabulous drunken British lady. It was considerably past my bedtime, and the whole scene was starting to bum me out. I stood next to my friend Zoe, who, at only four, was an embar-rassingly juvenile companion. The British lady, trying to make conversation, asked Zoe and me what our parents did if we were "bad girls."

"When I'm bad, I get a time-out," Zoe said.

"When I'm bad," I announced, "my father sticks a fork in my vagina."

This is hard to share without alarm bells sounding. We're taught to listen to little girls, particularly when they say things about being sodomized with cutlery. Also my father makes sexually explicit artwork so he's probably already on the FBI's fork-in-vagina radar. It's a testament to his good nature that, after the British lady repeated my "hilarious" story to a group of adults, he simply scooped me up and said, "I think it's someone's bedtime."

It's hard to grasp what my intent was here—we're talking about a child who was fond of pretending a ghost was touching her nonbreasts against her will—but I guess the moral of this story is that my dad's really nice, yet I've always had an imagination that could grasp, maybe even appreciate, the punitive.

There is a theory not often discussed—perhaps because I'm the inventor of the theory—that if your father is incredibly kind, you will seek an opposite relationship as an act of rebellion.

Nothing about my history would imply that I'd dig jerks. I went to my first Women's Action Coalition meeting at age three. We, the daughters of downtown rabble-rousers, sat in a back room, coloring in line drawings of Susan B. Anthony while our mothers plotted their next demonstration. I understood that feminism was a worthy concept long before I was aware of being female, listening to my mother and her friends discuss the challenges of navigating the male-dominated art world. My feminist indoctrination continued at forward-thinking private schools where gender inequality was as much a topic of study as algebra, at all-girls camp in Maine, and as I looked through my grandmother's wartime photo albums ("Nurses did the *real* work," she always said). And underscoring it all was my father's insistence that my sister and I were the prettiest, smartest, and baddest bitches in Gotham town, no matter how many times we pissed ourselves or cut our own bangs with blunt kitchen scissors.

I don't think I met a Republican until I was nineteen, when I shared an ill-fated evening of lovemaking with our campus's resident conservative, who wore purple cowboy boots and hosted a radio show called *Real Talk with Jimbo*. All I knew when I stumbled home from a party behind him was that he was sullen, thuggish, and a poor loser at poker. How that led to intercourse was a study in the way revulsion can quickly become desire when mixed with the right muscle relaxants. Midintercourse on the moldy dorm rug, I looked up into my roommate Sarah's potted plant and noticed something dangling. I tried to make out its shape, and then I realized—it was the condom. Mr. Face for Radio had flung the prophylactic into our tiny palm tree, thinking I was too dumb, drunk, or eager to call him on it.

"I think . . . ? The condom's . . . ? In the tree?" I muttered feverishly.

"Oh," he said, like he was as shocked as I was. He reached for it as if he was going to put it back on, but I was already up, stumbling toward my couch, which was the closest thing to a garment I could find. I told him he should probably go, chucking his hoodie and boots out the door with him. The next morning, I sat in a shallow bath for half an hour like someone in one of those coming-of-age movies.

He didn't say hi to me on campus the next day, and I didn't even know if I wanted him to. He graduated in December, and with him so did 86 percent of Oberlin's Republican population. I channeled my feelings of shame into a short experimental film called *Condom in a Tree* (a classic!) and determined that the next time I was penetrated it would be a more respectful situation.

That's when I met Geoff.

Geoff was a senior, a fair-haired meditator who once cried in my parents' hammock because, he told me, "You are forcing sex when I just want to be heard." He had his low points.*  But for the most part, he nurtured and supported me. We loved each other in a calm, gentle, and equal way. Geoff was not a jerk, but he also wasn't for me.

We broke up, as most college couples do. I spent the next month bedridden, unable to stomach anything but mac and cheese. Even my patient father grew tired of my cartoonish heartbreak. But at my first postcollege job in a downtown restaurant, I met a different kind of guy. Joaquin was almost ten years older than me, born in Philadelphia, and possessed a swagger that seemed unearned, considering he was wearing a FUCKING FEDORA. His body was long and lean, and he dressed like Marlon Brando in *Streetcar*. He was my overlord, a cynical foodie whose favorite maxims included "It would suck to live past forty-five." Even though he had a girlfriend, we flirted. The flirting consisted of him questioning my general intelligence and noting my lack of spatial aware-

---

*• The time we took ecstasy and, right before it hit, he asked me what my thoughts on open relationships were. Cut to twelve hours of sobbing, not the eight-hour orgasm my friend Sophie had described.

• The time he made me drive three hours to his friend's birthday party, then was too socially anxious to enter it.

• The time he invented a purple cat that lived in his cupboard and made general mischief. Or was this a high point?

ness and then winking to let me know it was all in good fun. One night someone took a shit not in the toilet but on the floor in front of it.

"I hope you know you're cleaning that up," he said.

I didn't do it, but I sort of liked being told to. Joaquin was absolutely impertinent and, despite my "why I oughta!" faux consternation, I was melting. He was Snidely Whiplash, and I was the innocent girl tied to the tracks, but I didn't want Dudley Do-Right to come.

We started emailing. Mine were long and overwrought, trying to show him how dark my sense of humor was (I can make an incest joke!) and how much I knew about Roman Polanski. His were brief, and I could read both nothing and everything into them. He never even signed his name. On the night I quit, we met after work and smoked some pot I had hunted down specifically for the occasion. I didn't have rolling papers (because I didn't smoke pot!) so we wrapped it in a page of *Final Cut Pro for Dummies*. When I tried to kiss him, he told me he shouldn't—not because he had a girlfriend, but because he was already sleeping with a different hostess. We went out to a twenty-four-hour Pakistani restaurant and, having been rejected, I was hungry for the first time in days. We ate our naan in silence.

We maintained our version of a friendship until finally, the following June, we kissed in the street outside the restaurant. I was disappointed by how hard his lips were and how silent he was once he had an erection.

What followed was two years of on-and-off ambiguous sex hangouts, increasingly perverse in their execution and often involving prescription drugs I'd hoarded from my parents' various oral surgeries. He'd ignore me for months on end, during which time

I'd ride the subway in a beret imagining I saw him getting on at every stop. When he did invite me over, his house was a suckhole. If I fell asleep there, it was often noon the next day before I got out the door. In the street I'd blink at the flat Brooklyn sunlight, cold to my bones.

This relationship culminated in the worst trip to Los Angeles ever seen outside of a David Lynch film. We spent four days in the Chateau Marmont, where John Belushi's ghost makes the tub run funny and they're mean to you if you ask for a spoon. Highlights included him never touching me once, me falling asleep wearing only a thigh-high boot that belonged to my mother, and his confession that he didn't think he knew how to care about another person.

As I gained some traction in my creative pursuits, I thought his respect for me would grow, but all it did was provide me with more money to slip out of dinner with friends and take a cab to his house. I hoped nobody asked me where I was going so I wouldn't be forced to lie. We had sex one or two times after our LA excursion, but my heart wasn't in it. If my heart was even in it before.

If I was writing this then, I would have glamorized the whole story for you—told you how misunderstood Joaquin was and how he was just as sad, scared, and lonely as the rest of us. I would have laughed as I described all the weird sexual liberties I let him take and his general immaturity (unassembled bed frame blocking the front door, cigar box full of cash, condoms in random pockets). Before entering Joaquin's house I always reminded myself that this wasn't exactly where I was meant to be, but pit stops are okay on the road of life, aren't they? I thought of myself as some kind of spy, undercover as a girl with low self-esteem, bringing back detailed intelligence reports on the dark side for girls with boyfriends who looked like lesbians and watched *Friday Night Lights* with them while eating takeout. They could have their supportive relationships and typical little love stories. I'd be Sid and Nancy–ing it up, refusing to settle for the status quo. I'd be cool.

I had a lucky little girlhood. It wasn't always easy to live inside my brain, but I had a family that loved me, and we didn't have to worry about much except what gallery to go to on Sunday and whether or not my child psychologist was helping with my sleep issues. Only when I got to college did it dawn on me that maybe my upbringing hadn't been very "real." One night outside my freshman dorm, a bunch of kids were smoking and shrieking with laughter, so I rushed outside in my pajamas, eager to join the fray.

"What's going on?" I asked.

"Oh," said Gary Pralick, who always wore a sweater knit by his great-grandmother (I later learned she was only seventy-nine). "Don't *you* worry about it, Little Lena from Soho."

What a snarky jerk. (Obviously, I later slept with him.) I tried my best to dismiss the comment, but it nagged at me, crept in during that nightly moment between eating three slices of pizza and being asleep. What was it that I couldn't understand and how could I understand it, short of moving to a war-torn nation? I couldn't escape the feeling that I had experiences to gain, things to learn. That feeling was the crux of my whole relationship with Joaquin.

Well, friends, learning about the "world" is not pretending you're a hooker while a guy from the part of New Jersey that's near Pennsylvania decides which Steely Dan record to put on at 4:00 A.M. The secrets of life aren't being revealed when someone laughs at you for having studied creative writing.

There is no enlightenment to be gained from letting your semiboyfriend's bald friend touch your thigh too close to the place where it meets your crotch, but you let it happen because you think you might be in love. How else can you explain why you've spent so much money getting to his house?

The first few times Joaquin and I had sex, it was quick and a little sad. The overhead lights buzzed. He didn't look at me, and afterward he didn't linger. I wondered if it was somehow my fault. Maybe I was a dead fish, uncreative in the sack, paralyzed by my desperation to please. Maybe I was destined to lie there like a slab until I was too old for intercourse.

Then, the night before Thanksgiving, I met him at a bar in Queens. Wearing fishnets and a little gray skirt-suit from J. C. Penney, I was dressed like a hooker dressed as an insurance broker. But something about the outfit inspired him, and he looked at me with a new kind of hunger that drove us back toward his house, where he kissed me on the couch, determined, maybe a little pissed. He guided me to the bed, where he turned me on my stomach. Alcohol, fear, and fascination cloud my memory, but I know my tights were balled up and placed in my mouth. I didn't know where he was in the room at certain points, until I did. And he spoke to me, unleashing streams of the filthiest shit I had ever heard leave another human's mouth. Impressive in its narrative intricacy, and horrifying in its predilections. This, I decided to believe, is the best game I've ever played.

I walked out into the street the next day bare legged and reeling, not sure whether I'd been ruined or awoken.

But I got no closer to enlightenment hiding in a bodega down the block from Joaquin's house, pretending to be at a cool party "kinda near your place." He was busy. With his other girlfriend, who, he told me, was "very well raised and even her dirty underwear smells clean." Why did I keep calling? Because I was waiting for his mind to change, for him to talk to me the way my father does or the way Geoff did, even in our darkest hour. Intrigued as I was by this new dynamic of disrespect, at my core I didn't want to be spoken to like that. It made me feel silenced, lonely, and far away from myself, a feeling that I believe, next to extreme nausea sans vomiting, is the depth of human misery.

The end never comes when you think it will. It's always ten steps past the worst moment, then a weird turn to the left. After a long post-California cooling-off period, Joaquin and I fell in love for a week. At least that's what it felt like. It was October, still warm, with a near-constant drizzle. I had a new leather blazer, bought with my first paycheck. With its silver grommets and wide lapel, it made every outfit feel like a uniform from the future. We met for drinks, and he hugged me tightly. We talked about Los Angeles, how sad it had gotten, and the fact that we were better off as friends. We lingered, drink after drink, then at his house we agreed friends could have intercourse if they didn't kiss at all, *Pretty Woman* style. The next morning he rolled toward me and not away. He texted a few hours later to say he'd enjoyed the evening. It was like a miracle.

Two days later we met for a movie. I wore the jacket again, and he bought me a hamburger—he is the one who ended my vegetarian streak, for which I will be forever grateful because I grow strong on the blood of animals. He walked close to me, and I realized it was the first time he'd taken ownership of me in the street. Back in my bedroom at my house—my parents were away—we laughed and talked and returned to kissing. This is what it could have been like. This is what it had never been like. And so I was angry.

Emboldened by my new life as a woman with a meaningful job and a good jacket, I told Joaquin to fuck off forever. Well,

I told him via the Internet. After the best night we had ever had, the first night he'd let me feel like myself, I wrote him an email saying he had hurt me, taken advantage of my affection, and made me feel disposable. I told him that wasn't a way I was interested in being treated and that I wouldn't be available any longer. And then I made myself sick to my stomach waiting for an apology that never came.

After sending that email, I only slept in his bed one more time, wearing a full sweatsuit. Baby steps.

◆

When I'm playing a character, I am never allowed to explicitly state the takeaway message of the scenes I'm performing—after all, part of the dramatic conflict is that the person I'm portraying doesn't really know it yet. So let me do it here: I thought that I was smart enough, practical enough, to separate what Joaquin said I was from what I knew I was. The way I saw it, I was fully capable of being treated with indifference that bordered on disdain while maintaining a strong sense of self-respect. I obeyed his commands, sure that I could fulfill this role while still protecting the sacred place inside of me that knew I deserved more. Different. Better.

But that isn't how it works. When someone shows you how little you mean to them and you keep coming back for more, before you know it you start to mean less to yourself. You are not made up of compartments! You are one whole person! What gets said to you gets said to *all* of you, ditto what gets done. Being treated like shit is not an amusing game or a transgressive intellectual experiment. It's something you accept, condone, and learn to believe you deserve. This is so simple. But I tried so hard to make it complicated.

I told myself I'd asked for it. After all, Joaquin never said he'd break up with his girlfriend. He let me know from the start that he was a rebel and a tell-it-like-it-is-onator. He never even told me he'd call. But I also think when we embark on intimate relationships, we make a basic human promise to be decent, to hold a flattering mirror up to each other, to be respectful as we explore each other. As a friend recently complained to me of the lawyer she was dating: "How could someone who cares so much about social justice care so little about my feelings?" I told her about my belief in this promise. That it is right, and it is real. Joaquin didn't keep up his end of the bargain. And I didn't learn anything about life that I hadn't learned in Soho.

# *Barry*

I'M AN UNRELIABLE NARRATOR.

Because I add an invented detail to almost every story I tell about my mother. Because my sister claims every memory we "share" has been fabricated by me to impress a crowd. Because I get "sick" a lot. Because I use the same low "duhhh" voice for every guy I've ever known, except for the put-off adult voice I use to imitate my dad. But mostly because in another essay in this book I describe a sexual encounter with a mustachioed campus Republican as the upsetting but educational choice of a girl who was new to sex when, in fact, it didn't feel like a choice at all.

I've told the story to myself in different variations—there are a few versions of it rattling around in my memory, even though the nature of events is that they only happen once and in one way. The day after, every detail was crisp (or as crisp as anything can be when the act was committed in a haze of warm beer, Xanax bits, and poorly administered cocaine). Within weeks, it was a memory I turned away from, like the time I came around the corner of the funeral home and saw my grandpa laid out in an open coffin in his navy uniform.

The latest version is that I remember the parts I can remember. I wake up into it. I don't remember it starting, and then we are all over the carpet, Barry and I, no clear geography to the act. In the dusty half-light of a college-owned apartment I see a pale, flaccid penis coming toward my face and the feeling of air and lips in places I didn't know were exposed. The refrain I hear again and again in my head, a self-soothing mechanism of sorts, is: *This is what grown-ups do.*

In my life I've had two moments when I felt cool, and both involved being new in school. The first time was in seventh grade, when I switched from a Quaker school in Manhattan to an arts school in Brooklyn. At Quaker school I had been a vague irritant, the equivalent of a musical-theater kid, only I couldn't sing, just read the Barbra Streisand biography and ate prosciutto sandwiches, alone in my corner of the cafeteria, relishing solitude like a divorcée at a sidewalk café in Rome. But at my new school, I was cool. My hair was highlighted. I had platform shoes. I had a denim jacket and a novelty pin that said WHO LIT THE FUSE ON YOUR TAMPON? Boys had other boys come up to me and tell me they liked me. I told one Chase Dixon, computer expert with lesbian moms, that I just wasn't ready to be in a relationship. People loved my poetry. But after a little while, the sheen of newness faded, and I was, once again, just a B- or even C-level member of the classroom ecology.

The second time I was cool was when I transferred colleges, fleeing a disastrous situation at a school ten blocks from my home to a liberal arts haven in the cornfields of Ohio. I was again blond, again in possession of a stylish jacket—this one a smart green-and-white-striped peacoat made in Japan—and I was showered with attention by people who also seemed to like my poetry.

One of my first self-defining acts, upon arrival, was to join the staff of *The Grape*, a publication that took undue pride in being the alternative newspaper at an alternative college. I wrote porn reviews (*"Anal Annie and the Willing Husbands* is weird because the lead has a lisp"), scathing indictments of Facebook culture ("Stephan Markowitz's party journal is meant to make freshmen feel alone"), and a hard-hitting investigative report on the flooding of the Afrikan Heritage House dorm. One of the editors at the paper, Mike, intrigued me immediately, a six-foot-four senior with Napoleon Dynamite glasses but the swagger of a frat boy and the darkness of Ryan Gosling. He lived in Renson Cottage, a campus-owned Victorian famous for having been the college home of Liz Phair.

Toward the beginning of my *Grape* career Mike and I dirty-danced at a party, his knee wedged deep between my legs, a fact he seemed not to remember at the next staff meeting. He ran *The Grape* with an iron fist, verbally abusing underlings right and left, but I passed muster and he often invited me to sit with him in the cafeteria, where he and his tiny Jewish sidekick, Goldblatt, ate plates piled high with lo mein, veggie burgers, and every kind of dry, dry cake. Mike and I were engaged in a constant war of words. It was flirtatious. We worked hard to impress and even harder to seem like we didn't care.

"I don't think monogamy can ever work," he told me one day as we were meeting over cafeteria hash browns.

"I don't care. I'm not your girlfriend," I said.

"And thank God for that, toots."

I giggled. I was something far cooler than a girlfriend. I was a reporter. A temptress. A sophomore.

.  o⎯⎯o  .

That winter, I went home for a month with mono, and during that time Mike checked in with me often, under the pretense that he was "struggling, missing my A team over here" and getting pulverized by our rival, *The Oberlin Review*. On the night of my return, glands still swollen, I wore a vintage wedding dress to dinner with him and Goldblatt at the nicest restaurant in town. Mike smiled at me like we were a real couple (a couple that brought a tiny Jewish sidekick everywhere we went).

A few weeks later Mike came over to my room to watch *Straw Dogs*. I told him how disturbed I was by its depiction of female sexuality, of a woman who hated being coveted and really wanted to be taken advantage of, and then he lay on top of me and we kissed for forty minutes.

What followed was a torturous affair that resulted in, by the numbers:

One and a half rounds of intercourse
One shared shower (my first)
About seven brokenhearted poems that described
    the way "our bellies slapped together that night"
One very unnecessary pregnancy test

And one time I showed up to a party he was having with a red running nose and residual mono symptoms, begged him to talk to me in a corner, then fainted. I was carried home by his roommate Kyle, who encouraged me to respect myself.

When I was seven I learned the word "rape," but I thought it was "rabe." I pronounced it like the playwright, not the broccoli, and I used it with reckless abandon. One afternoon as I read on the couch, my two-year-old sister toddled over to me, her balloon-printed pajamas saggy in the butt from a dirty diaper. Oh, the injustice of having to live with a *child*. Grace, wanting desperately to play, grabbed at my feet and ankles. When that failed to elicit a reaction, she began to climb me like a jungle gym, giggling that baby giggle.

"Mom! Papa!" I screamed. "She's rabing me! She's rabing me!"

*"What?"* my mother asked, desperately trying to keep her lips from curling into a smile.

"Grace is rabing me."

Mike was the first person to go down on me, after a party to benefit Palestine, on my dorm room rug. I felt like I was being chewed on by a child that wasn't mine. The first time we had sex was the second time I'd ever done it. He put on some African music, kissed me like it was a boring job given to him by his parole officer, and I clung to him, figuring he'd let me know if this wasn't what sex was supposed to be like. When he finally came, he made little, scared-sounding noises like a cat stuck in the rain. I kept moving until he told me to stop.

·  🎩  ·

Noni and I are at the newsstand across from Grace's preschool, waiting for pickup. I am nine years old and have the
day off of school, which is my dream, but I haven't used it
well. Noni is my nanny. She is from Ireland and was in a bad
car accident when she was sixteen that made it so her jaw will
only open so far. Her hair is crispy from hairspray, and she
wears leggings that show her tan calves. We are looking at
magazines and drinking iced teas. The man who owns the
newsstand looks at me a moment, and for some reason it
sends a shiver down my spine.

"Noni," I whisper, panicked. "Noni."

She removes her head from her *People* magazine and leans
down to me. I know the real word now.

"What's doing?"

"I think he's trying to rape me."

·    ·

I helped Mike and Goldblatt buy finches for an installation
art project and, when they got loose in the bathroom of Renson Cottage, I used my experience as an Audubon volunteer
to corral the birds into a darkened corner and gather them
in my hands. The finch beat its wings, and I thought how
holding a small bird is the closest a nonsurgeon will come to
feeling a naked beating heart. The bird pecked at my hands,
but I'm not squeamish, and I shoved it back into the cage.
How many girls can do *that*?

·  🧊  ·

In May, Mike graduated along with his whole gang of merry bandits: Goldblatt, Kyle (an expert on Costa Rican culture), and Quinn, a textiles student whose senior project involved creating bathing suits with holes where the crotches should have been. The only one who was left behind was Barry. Barry would now be considered a super senior, a dubious distinction given to those with one more semester to finish.

Barry, Audrey and I agreed, was creepy. He had a mustache that rode the line between ironic Williamsburg fashion and big-buck hunter, and he wore the kind of white Reeboks last seen in an '80s exercise video. He worked part-time at the library, and I would often see him skulking along the aisles, shelving books in the wrong places. In social settings, he commanded attention with his aggressively masculine physicality and a voice that went Barry White low. There was a story about him punching a girl in the boobs at a party. He was a Republican. All reasons to avoid him and to wonder why they let him into the living room of Renson Cottage so much.

In his super-senior semester, Barry seemed lost. With his friends gone, his brow had softened. You could see him smoking cigarettes alone, kicking at the ground in front of the student union and sitting in Mike's old place in the computer lab like a dog without an owner.

Who's the big guy now?

There was a particularly raucous party in the loft above the video store. I wore Audrey's fancy wrap dress, and we drank two beers each before we left and split a Xanax she still had from a flight to Boca with her grandma. It hit me hard and fast, and by the time we showed up I was possessed by a party spirit quite alien to me. Audrey, on the other hand, became dizzy and after much deliberation went home, making me promise to treat her wrap dress with the proper respect. I missed her keenly for a moment, then snorted a small amount of cocaine off a key, before kissing a freshman and dancing into the bathroom line, where I showed people how easily Audrey's wrap dress opened and explained how "bogus" the creative writing department was.

All my friends were gone. I looked for Audrey, even though she'd told me she was leaving, and I'd also watched her go.

Finally, from behind, I saw my friend Joey. Sweet, oafish Joey—DJ and snugglebunny full of Michigan pride. There he was, in his Members Only jacket, tall and warm and ready to save me. I snuck up behind him and jumped on his back.

When he turned around, it wasn't Joey. It was Barry. *Uh-oh* played in my head like a loser's sound effect on a Japanese talk show. *Uh-oh uh-oh uh-oh.*

"I haven't seen you in a while," he said.

"Well, we don't know each other," I told him. "I have to pee."

Barry leads me to the parking lot. I tell him to look away. I pull down my tights to pee, and he jams a few of his fingers inside me, like he's trying to plug me up. I'm not sure whether I can't stop it or I don't want to.

Leaving the parking lot, I see my friend Fred. He spies Barry leading me by the arm toward my apartment (apparently I've told him where I live), and he calls out my name. I ignore him. When that doesn't work, he grabs me. Barry disappears for a minute, so it's just Fred and me.

"Don't do this," he says.

"You don't want to walk me home, so just leave me alone,"

I slur, expressing some deep hurt I didn't even know I had. "Just leave me alone."

He shakes his head. What can he do?

Now Barry's in my place.

Now we're on my floor, doing all the things grown-ups do. I don't know how we got here, but I refuse to believe it's an accident.

Now he's inside me, but he's only sort of hard. I look onto the floor, by his pale bent knee, and see he's taken off the condom. Did I tell him to wear a condom? The condom came from my first-aid kit. I knew where that was, he didn't, so I must have crawled for it. A choice. Why does he think it's okay to take it off?

I come to a little, realize this is not a dream. I tell him he has to put the condom back on. He's not hard, and now he's going down on me, and he's pushing his dick in my face. It feels like a finger without bones.

I moan, as if to say, *I like this, so much.*

He calls me baby. Or says, "Oh baby," which is different.

"Do you want to make me come?" I ask.

"Hunh?" he asks.

"Do you want to make me come?" I ask again, and I know that if I make these sounds and ask these questions, then it is, again, a choice.

Now we're across the room, our bodies in a new forma-tion. I tip my head back as far as it will go. And up, in my roommate's tree, I see another condom. Or the same con-dom. A condom that isn't on him and maybe never was.

Now I am pulling myself up messily like a just-born foal, throwing Barry and all his clothes out the sliding door into the parking lot. He's clutching his shirt, struggling with a boot. The winter air seems to sober him up, and I shut the door and watch from behind the glass as he looks for the direction home. I wouldn't want to run into him now. Now I am hiding in the kitchenette, waiting for him to be gone.

Now I wake up. My roommate isn't home. Later, I will learn she heard sounds from outside the door and went upstairs to sleep with a friend rather than interrupt me.

Before sunrise, I diligently enter the encounter into the Word document I keep, titled "Intimacy Database." *Barry. Number Four. We fucked. 69'd. It was terribly aggressive. Only once. No one came.*

When I was young, I read an article about a ten-year-old girl who was raped by a stranger on a dirt road. Now nearly forty, she recalled lying down in a gingham dress her mother had sewn for her and making sounds of pleasure to protect herself. It seemed terrifying and arousing and like a good escape plan. And I never forgot this story, but I didn't remember until many days after Barry fucked me. Fucked me so hard that the next morning I had to sit in a hot bath to soothe myself. Then I remembered.

The day after Barry, Audrey and I meet up to do homework in the computer lab. We are both still in our pajamas, layers and layers to guard against the cold. In the bathroom we are washing our hands, letting them linger in the hot water, and I say, "I have to tell you something." We crawl up onto the ledge above the radiator, and we huddle together, and I describe the events of the night before, finishing with "I'm sorry about your wrap dress."

Audrey's pale little face goes blank. She clutches my hand and, in a voice reserved for moms in Lifetime movies, whispers, "You were raped."

I burst out laughing.

That night I am Gchatting with Mike. He lives in San Francisco now, works at an ad agency, and dates a girl with a pill problem and what he calls "a phat ass." Her Myspace name is Rainbowmolly.

> **12:30 AM**
> **me:** fool
> i called you
> **Mike:** i know
> i've been hung ove
> r
> hungover
> **me:** me too
>
> **12:31 AM**
> **Mike:** REALLY
> **me:** i got so drunked up
> **Mike:** nice
> i vomited on myself
> **me:** ew
> are you ok?
> **Mike:** yes

**12:32 AM**
i haven't
left my house
**me:** i did something so retarded
you will laugh at me
**Mike:** tell me

**12:33 AM**
TELL ME
**me:** i went home with you weird friend Barry
**Mike:** --------------------
haha
HAHAHA
**me:** i know

I dial Mike on my hot-pink flip phone, not sure whether I want him to pick up or not. "How weird is that?"

"Well, Barry called me today, said he woke up in the hall-way of his dorm. Said he deep-dicked some girl, but he has no idea who." He laughs, a mucusy exhausted laugh.

"Deep-dicked" will never leave me. It will stay with me long after the sting inside me, like rug burn deep within my body, is gone. After I've forgotten the taste of Barry's bitter spit or the sound of him cursing through the thick glass of my sliding door. Divorced of meaning, it's a set of sounds that mean shame.

The next week my vagina still hurts. When I walk, when I sit. I thought a hot bath the morning after would cure it, but it's just getting worse. I'm home on winter break, freezing except for this hot place where nothing will settle down, so I go to my mother's doctor, the one who delivered my sister. Gently, she examines me and explains it is getting better slowly. It's like a scrape on your knee, a scab rubbing against jeans.

"It must have been pretty rough," she says without judgment.

The next semester, after Barry is gone, my friend Melody tells me that once her friend Julia woke up the morning after sex with Barry, and the wall was spattered with blood. *Spattered,* she said, "like a crime scene." But he was nice, and he took her for the morning-after pill and named the baby they weren't having. Julia wasn't mad. "But you should know," she says, "that he lost his virginity to a hooker in New Orleans."

What will I do with this retroactive warning? Just sit on it, what else can I do.

I make a vow not to have sex again until it's with someone I love. I wait six months, and the next person I do it with becomes my first serious boyfriend, and though he is sexually confused and extremely antisocial he treats me like the eighth wonder of the world and we are best friends.

One afternoon, lying in bed in a way that is only acceptable during college or a deep seasonal depression, I tell him about Barry. I cry, partially from remembering it and partially because I hate the way I'm expressing myself. He's really hung up on trying to remember whether he ever saw Barry around campus. I'm just angry that I don't have better words.

Even in the nicest television writers' room, people say all kinds of terrible things. Confessions of the way we really feel toward our significant others. Stories from our childhoods that our parents wish we had forgotten. Judgments of other people's bodies. It's all fodder for A and B stories, motivations, throwaway jokes. I wonder how many loved ones watch TV looking for signs of their own destruction.

We laugh a lot, at things that shouldn't rightfully be funny—breakups, overdoses, parents explaining their impending divorce to a little kid with chicken pox. That's the joy of it. One afternoon, I pitch a version of the Barry story. A sexual encounter that no one can classify properly. A condom winding up in a potted plant against the will of the girl being fucked. An Audrey-esque "ambulance chaser" response.

Murray shakes his head. "I just don't see rape being funny in any situation."

"Yeah," Bruce agrees. "It's a tough one."

"But that's the thing," I say. "No one *knows* if it's a rape. It's, like, a confusing situation that . . ." I trail off.

"But I'm sorry that happened to you," Jenni says. "I hate that."

. ⌐🖋 .

I tell Jack by accident. We're talking on the phone about unprotected sex, how it isn't good for people with our particular temperament, our anxiety like an incorrigible weed. He asks if I've had any sex that was "really stressful," and out the story comes, before I can even consider how to share it. Jack is upset. Angry, though not at me.

I'm crying, even though I don't want to. It's not cathartic, or helping me prove my point. I still make joke after joke, but my tears are betraying me, making me appear clear about my pain when I'm not. Jack is in Belgium. It's late there, he's so tired, and I'd rather not be having this conversation this way.

"It isn't your fault," he tells me, thinking it's what I need to hear. "There's no version of this where it's your fault."

I feel like there are fifty ways it's my fault. I fantasized. I took the big pill and the small pill, stuffed myself with substances to make being out in the world with people my own age a little bit easier. To lessen the space between me and everyone else. I was hungry to be seen. But I also know that at no moment did I consent to being handled that way. I never gave him permission to be rough, to stick himself inside me without a barrier between us. I never gave him permission. In my deepest self I know this, and the knowledge of it has kept me from sinking.

I curl up against the wall, wishing I hadn't told him. "I love you so much," he says. "I'm so sorry that happened."

Then his voice changes, from pity to something sharper.

"I have to tell you something, and I hope you'll understand."

"Yes?" I squeak.

"I can't wait to fuck you. I hope you know why I'm saying that. Because nothing's changed. I'm planning how I'm going to do it."

"You're going to do it?"

"All different ways."

I cry harder. "You better."

I have to go put on a denim vest for a promotional appearance at Levi's Haus of Strauss. I tell Jack I have to hang up now, and he moans "No" like I'm a babysitter wrenching him from the arms of his mother who is all dressed up for a party. He's sleepy now. I can hear it. Emotions are exhausting to have.

"I love you so much," I tell him, tearing up all over again.

I hang up and go to the mirror, prepared to see eyeliner dripping down my face, tracks through my blush and foundation. I'm in LA, so bring it on, universe: I can only expect to go down Lohan style. But I'm surprised to find that my face is intact, dewy even. Makeup is all where it ought to be.

I look all right. I look like myself.

## *Falling in Love*

*If you cut a piece of guitar string /*
*I would wear it like it's a wedding ring.*

—CARLY RAE JEPSEN

*He plays the guitar, this guy. Not professionally but, oh, it's*
*nice. Yes, I'm seeing him and he's laughing at me. He's so*
*funny. He's coming in April.*

—TERRY, my mom's psychic

I HAVE UTTERED THE WORDS "I love you" to precisely four
men, not including my father, uncle, and assorted platonic
neurotics I go to the movies with.

The first was my college boyfriend, whom I have tortured
enough in the public forum, so I will not rehash our affair

here. Suffice it to say, I told him first, and he did not reciprocate. It took weeks of crying and begging for him to reply in kind, and shortly after that he took it back. When he finally gave it again, the words had lost their charm.

The second "I love you" was Ben, a rebound from that relationship. I knew him from college, where we had slept together a few times before he ruined it all by getting into a freezing dorm shower, then hurling himself, nude, upon my unmade bed, screaming "I WANNA KNOW WHERE DA GOLD AT!" (He then ruined it further by ceasing contact with me.) But college ended, and I became lonely, as one does, and for the first time in my life *bored,* and soon I had maxed out my brand-new card on a plane ticket to the Bay Area, where he now lived on a block that was reminiscent of the credits of *Full House,* with big bay windows and a poster of the slain Mexican icon Selena on his yellowed bedroom wall. We spent four days trekking up and down hills, sitting on trolleys with our hands clasped, having drinks with guys who worked in bike shops, and coming together in sexual communion. One morning at breakfast, his roommate announced, "You two have sex like clockwork, once in the morning and once at night. Just like a married couple."

At night we sat on his back porch and ate the ravioli he'd spent all afternoon making by hand. He had a lot of time to cook: his job, editing the newsletter for a nonprofit that promoted the global language of Esperanto, was "flexible."

When he finally had to go to work, I visited friends on Telegraph Hill, where wild parrots live and where the view has the kind of urban grandeur that is incredibly satisfying to yuppies. This was before I had any conception of the financial reality of my friends. "Oh," I'd explain about a friend living in a massive West Village loft, "I think he makes tons of money at his internship for Food Not Bombs." It was only later that I realized these friends on Telegraph Hill, a film-maker and a poet, were house-sitting and couldn't actually afford a mansion with a roof shower. At the time, I marveled at what San Francisco real estate could provide for artists. If we worked hard enough, Ben and I could move up here, with a mutt and a bookshelf and a little orange smart car.

I cried when I had to go home, giving him a mix that included several obscure covers of "I Left My Heart in San Francisco."

Through the winter I dreamed of my new life out west. Ben sent pictures of pancakes and sunglasses from the dollar store and of parties where hippies parked boats in their living room. New tattoos of dollar signs and Communist symbols. Help-wanted postings from sex shops and children's literacy programs. He mailed me a tin of brownies with a note that was ironically signed "platonic regardz, Ben."

I came back again on a Friday afternoon, and he met me at the airport. We took the BART to his house, which is sort of like the New York subway system only you can apparently trust the people of San Francisco to respect upholstered seating. As we sat, smiling and satisfied, an old Chinese woman passed and hocked a loogie on his shoe. "Oy, bitch!" he yelled. Surprising myself, I secretly sided with her.

On Sunday, a homeless man camouflaged as a bush jumped out at me on the pier, laughed when I screamed, then demanded money. Ben seemed impressed with his ingenuity. Later, Ben removed the Selena poster from the wall so he could snort Adderall off her breasts. I got a terrible cold and couldn't find anything resembling a tissue in the apartment. Both of our credit cards were declined at the health-food store.

Wherever you go, there you are.

The night he told me he loved me, he was sloppy drunk.

We were in his bedroom, and I was straddling him in his desk chair, listening to a party winding down in the living room, when he blurted it out. I declined to answer him until I was beneath him in bed ten minutes later. He told me that *"I love you"* during sex doesn't count. The next day we ate too much In-N-Out Burger (we were both kind of fat, which at the time seemed like a revolution) and lay in bed beside each other and I cried, ostensibly because I'd miss him when I left but truly because I felt dead inside.

I did love Ben, in a sense. Because he cooked for me. Because he told me that my body was beautiful, like a Renaissance painting, something I badly needed to hear. Because his stepmother was the same age as him, and that is really sad. But I also didn't: Because his vanity drove him to wear vintage shoes that gave him blisters. Because he gave me HPV.

He called me terrible names when I broke up with him for a Puerto Rican named Joe with a tattoo that said MOM in Comic Sans. Admittedly, I didn't handle it too well either when, several months later, he moved in with a girl who taught special-needs preschool. I didn't utter the words "I love you" again in a romantic context for more than two years. Joe turned out to consider blow jobs misogynistic and pretended his house had caught fire just to get out of plans.

The third "I love you" was said to Devon. I was nearly done shooting the first season of *Girls*, and I had entertained a few crushes throughout the duration of production. One was on our assistant property master, a meek bespectacled fellow named Tom, who, I eventually concluded, was a lot stupider than he looked. Next I set my sights on an actor with the face of a British soccer hooligan. He took me to a bar on Eleventh Street, cried about his former fiancée, tongued me against a lamppost, then told me he didn't want a relationship.

It wasn't just that these crushes made the days pass quicker or satisfied some raging summer lust. On some deeper level, they made it all feel less adult. I'd been thrust into a world of obligations and responsibilities, budgets and scrutiny. My creative process had gone from being largely solitary to being witnessed by dozens of "adults" who I was sure were waiting to shout *This! This is the reason we don't hire twenty-five-year-old girls!* Romance was the best way I knew to forget my obligations, to obliterate the self and pretend to be someone else.

Devon appeared on the set of *Girls* while I was directing the season finale. He was a friend of a friend, brought in as some additional manpower on a tough shoot day. Small and puckish, with a meaty Neanderthal brow, he threw sandbags around with deceptive ease and coiled cables like an expert. I noticed a piercing in the cartilage of his right ear (so '90s), and I liked the way his jeans nestled in the top of his pristinely maintained work boots. When he smiled it was a mean little smile that revealed a gap between his two front teeth. After several interactions in which he questioned my authority and pretended not to hear me speaking, it was clear he was my type.

When Devon arrived I was in the middle of a full dissociative meltdown. The anxiety that has followed me through my life like a bad friend had reappeared with a vengeance and taken a brand-new form. I felt like I was outside my own body, watching myself work. I didn't care if I succeeded or failed because I wasn't totally sure I was alive. Between scenes I hid in the bathroom and prayed for the ability to cry, a sure sign I was real. I didn't know why this was happening. The cruel reality of anxiety is that you never quite do. At the moments it should logically strike, I am fit as a fiddle. On a lazy afternoon, I am seized by a cold dread. In this moment I had plenty to be anxious about: pressure, exposure, a tense argument with a beloved colleague. But I had even more to be thankful for.

Yet I couldn't feel anything.

Three days later he showed up at our wrap party. His arms were as muscly as a Ken doll's but also as small. I ignored his presence, mingling with my cast mates and drinking a thimble or so of red wine (which is enough to get me wasted). Eventually, sloshed and sure the evening held no other prospects, I sat down beside him at the bar and announced, "You're rude and I think you have a crush on me."

A few minutes of unremarkable conversation passed before he leaned in and lowered his tone. "Here's what's going to happen," he said. "I'm going to leave and wait on the corner. You're going to wait three minutes, then you're going to leave. You're not going to say goodbye to anyone and we're going to take a cab to my house."

I was struck by the tidiness of the plan. After months of frantic decision making, it was such a relief to have it laid out for me.

I tried to kiss him on the walk to the cab, and he held me off. "Not yet," he said. In the cab his credit card didn't work, and I paid drunkenly and showily. I followed him up the stairs to his fourth-floor walk-up. When he opened the door, he called out: "Nina? Joanne? Emily?" His roommates, he explained. As he turned the lights on, it became apparent we were in a studio apartment. No girls lived here. We were alone. I laughed too hard.

Before he would kiss me, he had to pack his bag for a job the next day. I watched as he carefully filled a backpack with tools, checked to make sure his power drill was charged, and examined his call sheet for details. I liked the careful obsessive way he prepared to do his job. It reminded me of my father teaching me to wash dishes. His room was painted red and didn't have a window. I sat on the bed and waited.

After what felt like months, he sat across from me, one foot still on the floor, and looked at me a long moment, like he was preparing to eat something he wasn't sure he would like. I wasn't offended. I wasn't even sure I was real. When we kissed it was dizzying. I fell back, unsure of where I was or what was happening, knowing only that the part of me that had left had come back, and the reattachment was almost painful, Wendy attempting to sew Peter Pan's shadow to his body. I was amazed by the fluidity of Devon's movements, how slick it was when he reached for the condom, reached for me, reached for the light to make it dark.

When we had sex, he was silent, and that, along with the pitch black, created the impression that I was being penetrated by a succubus of some kind. He felt oddly far away, and when I asked for confirmation of his name, he would give none. The next morning I awoke with a horrible feeling he was called Dave.

We spent the rest of the week together. I'd finish work and go straight to his house. We would talk—about movies he hated, books he was okay with, and people he avoided. His misanthropic spirit was apparent in everything he said and did.

"I like you," I told him on the third night, sitting between his knees, up past my bedtime.

"I know you do," he said.

He was odd, certainly. He kept his shower cap on the ceiling on a pulley he had rigged so he could lower it whenever it was needed. He had only orange juice in his fridge, and Hershey's chocolate "because that's what girls like." He kept matches by his toilet for when he shit, which seemed both

polite and tragic due to the amount of time he'd been spending alone. He spoke of his high-school ex with the kind of
lingering bitterness more often felt by husbands who have
been abandoned and left to care for multiple children.

After that week, I had to go. To LA, to work. He wasn't an
excuse to stay, even though he felt like one. He walked me to
the subway, and I headed to the airport, teary-eyed. I was myself again, and I didn't like it.

The rest of our relationship (five months) went swiftly
downhill. His critical nature proved suffocating—he hated
my skirts, my friends, and my work. He hated rom-coms and
just plain coms. He hated Thai food and air-conditioning
and "whiny" memoirs. What had initially seemed like a deep
well of pain caused by unattainable women was actually a
Philip Rothian disdain for the fairer sex. It's become horribly
and offensively popular to say that someone is on the autism
spectrum, so all I'll say is his inability to notice when I was
crying had to be some kind of pathology.

We spent torturous weekends attempting to share brunches
and movie dates like people who knew each other. But he
wasn't impressed enough by how funny my dad is, and I
didn't understand what was so cool about his friend Leo the
puppeteer. I attempted to break up with him on no fewer
than seven occasions, and each time he would cry, beg, and
show more emotion than he ever had during our silent sexual encounters or our mornings drinking tea in bed. "You
care about me," he'd tell me. "You've never felt like this before." And who was I to object?

I hauled Devon a lot of places I shouldn't have, in an attempt to make him a part of my life: dinner with girlfriends,
the Christmas tree at the Met, even a family vacation to Germany. (My father asked me to reconsider. I was so afraid on

the plane headed there that I took two Klonopin and bought all new luggage on my layover.)

"You can't draw blood from a stone," my mother told me—gently, considering she'd had to tend to him for almost five hours one afternoon while I sat in the hotel room contemplating my fate. If I ended this, would I be alone forever? Sure, he hated my skirts. Sure, he wrote fiction about what sluts the girls who work at J.Crew are. But what of love?

· ♥ ·

My parents fell in love when they were twenty-seven. It was 1977, and they both lived downtown and ran with the same crowd of artists who wore Chinese slippers and played tennis ironically. My father framed pictures, and my mother took them, and so she asked him to help her, and the rest is history.

"Tell me again about how you met Mom," I ask my father.

"Not if you're just going to write about it," he says. But ultimately he can't resist—describing how odd her sense of humor was and how impossibly dramatic her friends were. "They just walked around starting fights with people."

The story has everything: drama, jealousy, drunkenness, friendships ended, and cats inherited. He liked the way she dressed, a little mannish, and the way she carried herself—same. She had revised her original opinion of him, which was that he looked just like a mouse. They had no cell phones so had to make plans and keep them or walk over to each other's houses and ring the bell and hope for the best. Sometimes he got drunk and made her angry. Sometimes she started fights just because she was hungry. Sometimes they went to parties and watched each other across smoky lofts, amazed. Despite different genetics and cultural affiliations, they had identical coloring, were about the same height. Weighed the same amount, too. Like long-lost siblings. I love imagining them then, knowing no more than I do, just that they liked the way it felt to be together.

· ♡ ·

Devon didn't fix that dissociated feeling for good, and when it came back, it came back harder. I had broken up with him on my seventh try, and one try didn't even count because all I could muster was "I love you."

"I know you do," he said. But he was wrong.

I lay in bed all day, rubbing my feet together and whispering, "You are real. You are real. You are . . ."

And when I emerged, fifteen pounds lighter but too shaken to enjoy it, I thought, I could spend the next eight years just getting to know myself and that would be fine. The idea of sex right now sounds about as appealing as putting a live lobster *up there*.

· ♪ ·

Then he appeared. Gap toothed, Sculpey faced, glasses like a cartoon, so earnest I was suspicious, and so witty I was scared. I saw him standing there, yellow cardigan and hunched shoulders, and thought: Look, there is my friend. The next months were a lesson in opening up, letting go, being kind and brave.

I have written all sorts of paragraphs recounting those months together: first kiss, first Mister Softee, first time I noticed that he won't touch a doorknob without covering his hand with his sweatshirt. I have written sentences about how the first time we made love it felt like dropping my keys on the table after a long trip, and about wearing his sneakers as we ran across the park toward my house, which would someday be our house. About the way he  gathered me up after a long terrible day and put me to bed. About the fact that he is my family now. I wrote it down, found the words that evoked the exact feeling of the edge of the park at 11:00 P.M. on a hot Tuesday with the man I was starting to love. But surveying those words I realized they are mine. He is mine to protect. There is so much I've shared, and so much that's been crushed by the sharing. I never mourned it, because it never mattered.

· ⬡ ·

I don't love any of my old boyfriends anymore. I'm not sure I ever did, and I'm not sure if at the time I thought I was sure. My mother says that's normal, that men are proud of every one of their conquests, and women wish they could forget it all. She says that's an essential gender difference, and I can't say I disprove her theory. What keeps me from full revulsion, from wanting the sexual equivalent of an annulment, is thinking about what I got from each one that I still hold on to now.

My college boyfriend got me more in touch with my gut health (both a blessing and a curse) and made me ask some larger questions about the universe that I had been ignoring in favor of buying *US Weekly* the moment it hit the stands every Wednesday.

Ben taught me the term "self-actualized," and it became not just a favorite phrase but a goal.

Devon made me a pencil case with a built-in sharpener, lent me his watch, showed me how to keep all my wires from getting tangled, and changed my iPhone alarm from marimba to timba so that I wake up happier, more soothed.

And now I come to him, whole and ready to be known differently. Life is long, people change, I would never be foolish enough to think otherwise. But no matter what, nothing can ever be as it was. Everything has changed in a way that sounds trite and borderline offensive when recounted over coffee. I can never be who I was. I can simply watch her with sympathy, understanding, and some measure of awe. There she goes, backpack on, headed for the subway or the airport. She did her best with her eyeliner. She learned a new word she wants to try out on you. She is ambling along. She is looking for it.

# SECTION II
# *Body*

LENA
dans
Le Bain

# "Diet" Is a Four-Letter Word

*How to Remain 10 Lbs. Overweight*
*Eating Only Health Food*

AS A CHILD I developed a terrible fear of being anorexic. This was brought on by an article I had read in a teen magazine, which was accompanied by some upsetting images of emaciated girls with hollow eyes and folded hands. Anorexia sounded horrible: you were hungry and sad and bony, and yet every time you looked in the mirror at your eighty-pound frame, you saw a fat girl looking back at you. If you took it too far, you had to go to a hospital, away from your parents. The article described anorexia as an epidemic spreading across the nation, like the flu or the *E. coli* you could get from eating a Jack in the Box hamburger. So I sat at the kitchen counter, eating my dinner and hoping I wasn't next. Over and over, my mother tried to explain that you didn't just *become* anorexic overnight.

Did I feel that instinct, to stop eating? she wondered.

No. I really liked eating.

And why wouldn't I? My diet, up to that point, consisted entirely of organic hamburger patties, spinach-and-cheese ravioli (which I called grass ravioli), and pancakes my dad made in the shape of mice or guns. I was told that eating, really eating, was the only way to become big and strong and smart.

Because I was little. So little. Even though my favorite foods were: Doritos. Steak. Sara Lee pound cake (preferably still half frozen). Stouffer's French bread pepperoni pizzas, my Irish nanny's shepherd's pie, and huge hunks of goose-liver pâté, eaten with my bare hands as a snack. My mother denies having let me eat raw hamburger meat and drink a cup of vinegar, but I know that both happened. I wanted to taste it all.

When I was born I was very fat for a baby—eleven pounds (which sounds thin to me now). I had three chins and a stomach that drooped to one side of my stroller. I never crawled, just rolled, an early sign that I was going to be resistant to most exercise and any sexual position that didn't allow me to relax my back. But by my third birthday something began to change. My black hair fell out and grew in blond. My chins melted away. I walked into kindergarten as a tiny, tan little dreamboat. I can remember spending what must have been hours, as a kid, looking in the mirror, marveling at the beauty of my own features, the sharp line of my hip, the

downy hairs on my legs, my soft golden pony-tail. I still envy my own eight-year-old self, standing confidently on a Mexico beach in a French bikini, then breaking for nachos and Coke.

Then the summer after eighth grade I got

my period. My dad and I were taking a walk in the country when I felt something ticklish on my inner thigh. I looked down to see a thin trail of blood making its way toward my ankle sock.

"Papa?" I murmured.

His eyes welled up. "Well," he said, "in Pygmy cultures you'd have to start having children right about now."

He called my mother, who rushed home from her errands with a box of tampons and a meatball sub.

I soon gained thirty pounds. Starting high school is hard enough without all your favorite nightgowns becoming belly shirts. But here I was, a slip of a thing suddenly shaped like a gummy bear. I wasn't obese, but a senior did tell me I looked "like a bowling ball with a hat on." According to  my mother, some of it was hormonal. Some of it was the result of the medication that was keeping my obsessive-compulsive disorder in check. All of it was alien—and alienating.

This was the same year that I became a vegan. This was inspired by a love of puppies and also a cow who winked at me on a family vacation to Saint Vincent and the Grenadines. Rationally, I knew the cow was probably attempting to re-move a fly on its lid without the aid of arms. But the wink, that seemingly irrefutable sign of sentience, stirred some-thing in me—a fear of causing another creature pain, of not acknowledging their suffering.

I maintained the position for nearly ten years, occasion-ally lapsing into vegetarianism and beating myself up about it. When I was seventeen years old I even had a vegan din-ner party that was chronicled in the style section of *The New York Times*—headline: "A Crunchy Menu for a Youthful Crowd!"—and catered by a now-defunct establishment called the Veg-City Diner. I wore my grandmother's Dior, insisted

on shoelessness (leather was a no-no), and explained to the reporter that, while I didn't care much about the Iraq War, I was very concerned by our nation's casual attitude toward bovine murder.

While my veganism began as a deeply felt moral position, it soon morphed into a not-very-effective eating disorder. I never thought of it as a diet, but it *was* a way to limit the vast world of food that I had once loved so dearly—I had the feeling I could go mad if not given any boundaries. I'd be like that guy who drank the ocean and still wasn't satisfied.

I fell in love with Cathy comics one afternoon at my grandmother's house, flipping through the *Hartford Courant.* They weren't printed in *The New York Times,* our household's newspaper of choice. So every week after that my grandmother carefully snipped them out of her newspaper and mailed them to me, no note. I would savor them after school over half a box of cookies, laboring to understand each joke. Cathy liked food and cats. She couldn't resist a sale or a carbohydrate. No men seemed to care for her. I could relate. By the time I reached high school, I no longer read Cathy, but I did act like her. I am thinking particularly of a shower I took where the lower half of my body was under the running water and the upper half was laid out on the bath mat, eating a loaf of bread.*

College was an orgy of soy ice cream, overstuffed burritos, and bad midwestern pizza inhaled at 3:00 A.M. I didn't think

---

* Bread tends to be vegan.

very much about my weight or how food made me feel or the fact that what I ate might even be having an impact on how I looked. My friends and I seemed to be running a codependent overeaters' network.

"You NEED and DESERVE that brownie."

"Hey, are you going to finish that risotto?"

When a friend of my mom's who I didn't know very well died, I ate a massive panini, using grief management as my excuse.

I didn't get on a scale until a year after I graduated. I maintained the childlike perspective that weighing yourself was something you only did at the doctor's office—and if you were being offered a lollipop as compensation.

Occasionally I would walk into the kitchen in my underwear, stand sideways to display what I considered abs, and remark to my mother, "I think I'm losing weight." She would nod politely and return to organizing the Sondheim section of her iTunes library.

At my annual gynecological exam, they stuck me on the scale. "I think I'm around one hundred forty," I told the nurse, who nodded and smiled as she inched the numbers upward. It clunked, and thunked, until finally it settled at a hair below one hundred sixty.

"We'll say one hundred fifty-nine," she offered charitably.

One hundred fifty-nine? One hundred fifty-nine!? This couldn't be right. This wasn't me. This wasn't my body. This was a mistake.

"I think your scale is broken," I told her. "It wasn't like this at home."

On my way out I called my friend Isabel, hot and tearful. "I think I might have a thyroid problem," I cried. "Come over?"

Isabel sat in my kitchen eating turkey from the package,

listening patiently while I lay down on the marble countertop and moaned. "I am so fat. I am just growing and growing. I am going to be too big to fit through the door of any clubs."

"We don't *go* to any clubs," she said.

"But if we did, you would have to carry me on a domed silver tray, like a piece of pork." I grew defensive against my own judgment. "And anyway, one hundred sixty pounds is not *that* big. It's like thirty pounds bigger than most tall models."

So here I was, in the waiting room of my mother's nutritionist, Vinnie. After all these years, she had won.

A note about my parents: they have a variety of holistic professionals on call. One of my earliest memories is being clutched tightly by my mother's psychic Dmitri, who smelled of essential oils and walked around our house investigating "energies." He told me I was going to live well into my nineties while I was just trying to watch TGIF.

Vinnie was unintimidating—he spoke lovingly of the Staten Island home he shared with his mother—but he didn't spare me the rod when explaining that this weight gain wasn't, in fact, the result of a wayward thyroid.

No, it was a result of too much sugar. I had, I told him, been eating eleven tangerines a day. Not enough healthy fat. Mild anemia. General overeating. He gave me some great basic principles (eat protein, avoid sugar, have breakfast), and he made it clear that every time I ate a cookie or a hunk of baguette I was filling my body with unusable calories, unnecessary inflammation jamming my gears.

He told Isabel, who also wanted a tune-up, that the most digestible alcohol was champagne and that there's nothing wrong with eating a lot of olive oil. To my mind Isabel didn't need his help, considering she once lost twenty pounds eating an entire angel food cake per day and nothing else, but I was glad to have a comrade-in-arms. At Vinnie's urging, I began to keep track of what I consumed (down to the almond) in an iPhone app and lost nearly twenty pounds in a few months. I sat at my temp job, my snacks for the day lined up on the desk in front of me, waiting for the moment I could add them to my log. I both dreaded and cherished the last bite of the day (usually another almond). I couldn't see the difference in my body, but my scale, and my mother, assured me I was shrinking.

Every pound lost made me giddy, but at the same time a voice inside me screamed, *Who is this lady you've become? You are a potbellied riot girl! Why are you plugging your caloric intake into your smartphone!?*

What followed was a year of yo-yo dieting. Hence, this journal entry from the end of 2009: *I started to consider dieting and weight for the first time, going from 152 pounds to 145 pounds to 160 pounds to 142 pounds. Now, as I write this, I'm about 148 pounds and my goal is to reach 139 by February (but more on that later).*

Throughout much of that year, I was the world's least successful occasional bulimic. I understood the binging part of the equation fairly well, but after stuffing my face with all the readily available cookies and soy cheese I would drift into a stupor and forget to try and vomit. When I finally came to, all I could summon were dry heaves and a string of the celery I ate nine or ten hours ago, during a more hopeful time. My face puffy, my stomach aching, I'd fall asleep like a flu-y baby and awake the next morning with a vague awareness that something terrible had gone down between the hours of eleven thirty and one. Once my father noticed a constellation of broken capillaries around my eyes and asked me gently, "What the fuck did you do to your face?"

"I cried," I told him. "A lot."

Another time I announced my intention to puke up a box of pralines to my sister, who then banged on the locked bathroom door crying and screaming while I labored over the toilet. "It didn't even work," I told her, stalking back into my room.

A friend once told me that when you've been in AA, drinking is never fun again. And that's how I feel about having seen a nutritionist—I will never again approach food in an unbridled, guilt-free way. And that's okay, but I think of those college years as the time before I was expelled from Eden.

.　🦪　.

What follows are entries from a 2010 journal chronicling my attempts to lose weight. This has been, up until now, the most secret and humiliating document on my computer, kept more hidden than my list of passwords or my index of those I have encountered sexually.

### SATURDAY, AUGUST 21, 2010

**Breakfast, 11am:**

two pieces of gluten free toast (100 calories each)

w/ flax oil (120 calories)

¼ greek yogurt (35 calories)

peach (80 calories)

**lunch/snack, 1:30 p.m.:**

1 oz. salami (110 calories)

celery sticks (??)

**Afternoon snack, 3:30 p.m.:**

Mesa sunrise cereal (110 calories)
Rice dream (110 calories)
½ greek yogurt (25 calories)
w/ 8 pecans (104 calories)
8 dried cherries (30 calories)

**Dinner, 8:30 pm:**

Steamed zucchini (no calories?)
Approx 6 ounces steak (not sure of calories)
Tomatoes (60 calories?)
Arugula (3 calories?)
Newman's Own Dressing (45 calories)

**Dessert:**

Small bite dark chocolate (30 calories)
Swiss Miss Fat-Free Hot Cocoa (50 calories)

**4 am:**

1 bite of peach (10 calories)
spoonful chunky almond butter (110 calories)
celery (0 calories I think)

**total caloric intake:** approx: 1,560

**Notes:** could have had more veggies. I also recognize I look better than ever and that I'm radiating a kind of good health I haven't before. Also, working with my psychology/food guilt—the need to be perfect is what obsesses and then derails me, when the real goal is to enjoy food and listen to my body. That never steers me wrong. This journal is going to help a lot. I will try and stick to 1500 calories a day or less and not weigh myself next until September 22nd.

## SUNDAY, AUGUST 22, 2010

**Breakfast: 12:00 pm**

Mesa Sunrise cereal (120 calories)
Rice Dream (110 calories)
2 pecans (26 calories)
2 dried cherries (20 calories?)

**Lunch: 1:30 pm**

2 scrambled eggs with salsa (150 calories)
Arugula (3–7 calories)

**Snack: 3:45 pm**

¼ green apple (45 calories)
1 spoonful chunky almond butter (110 calories)
5 dried cherries (30 calories?)

**Snack: 6:40 pm**

⅔ bag of peeled fruit snack—dried fruits, cashews, walnuts
(200 calories)

**Dinner: 9pm**

2¼ corn chips with two scoops guacamole (100 calories?)
Chopped salad of beets, carrots, jicama, spinach, jalapeño
dressing (150 calories?)
Fried fish taco w/ corn tortilla (300 calories?)
1 piece of fried plantain (50 calories?)

**total caloric intake:** approx 1,411

**Notes:** This journal is a place to record all the conflicting, intense emotions I have about food and to free myself of them. It's about more than calories. I decided I will weigh myself every Sunday, so I know I'm on the right track. Today I weighed 149.5

on my mom's scale (a heavier scale). I'm not going to obsess about weight, but a positive goal would be to be 139 pounds by the November 12th premiere of *Tiny Furniture*. I am going to make strides to make that happen (taking my supplements, listening to my body, avoiding gluten, refined sugar, booze, a lot of red meat and fats, going to Physique 57 class even though the women there are all engaged to be married and mean).

## MONDAY, AUGUST 23RD, 2010

**1 am**

Smooth Move laxative tea

**Late night snack: 4:45 am**

Dried fruit (100 calories)

**Breakfast: 10:15 am**

1 Raweo raw chocolate cookie—these are like oreos but raw (100 calories)
2 fig/date/almond snowballs (180 calories)
1 tbsp Flax Oil (120 calories)
1 piece Tulu's gluten-free oat bread (120 calories?)
2 pieces leftover Chinese chicken (100 calories?)

**Lunch: 1:30 pm, Wild Ginger**

½ bowl vegetarian hot and sour soup (100 calories?)
Salad w/silken tofu and carrot-ginger dressing (200 calories?)
Steamed Chinese Broccoli (25 calories?)
Green tea (0 calories)

**Coffee: 3pm**

Coffee with ½ cup soy milk and tiny bit of maple syrup (50 calories?)

### Dinner: 6:30pm, Strip House

6-oz. filet mignon (348 calories)
½ serving creamed spinach (100 calories?)
EDITOR'S NOTE: yeah right
two bites fried potato (50 calories?)
1 bite toast w/bone marrow (60 calories?)
one bite escargot, ¼ snail (43 calories?)

### drinks:

2 seltzers

### total caloric intake: approx 1,576

**Notes:** I had diarrhea today! Maybe it's from the Smooth Move tea, which I am oddly addicted to. It tastes like chocolate!

### TUESDAY, AUGUST 24, 2010

### Breakfast: 10:30 a.m.

2 sugary cherries from a tart (20 calories?)
1 piece Tulu's gluten free honey oat bread (120 calories)
w/ almond butter (100 calories)
seltzer

### Lunch: 3 p.m.

Fruit salad w/ kiwi, orange, apple, grape, pineapple,
strawberry (110 calories)
Cottage cheese (100 calories)
Tea

### Dinner: 8:30 p.m.

Soy coconut pudding with berry sauce (300 calories?)
⅓ piece cornbread w. miso butter (100 calories?)

**Late Night Snack: 12:30 a.m.**

¼ piece cornbread with miso butter (150 calories?)
¼ cup ginger ale (93 calories?)

**total caloric intake:** approx 1,093

**Notes:** I have a bad fever (103) and general fluishness today. However, I do feel like I've hit a stride with my eating and I'm about 100% healthier mentally about it than I have been in a long time. Not swearing off of anything, or being extreme. Therefore, no desire to binge or go into a crazy food zone. It's a totally new sensation!

## WEDNESDAY AUGUST 25TH, 2010

### Breakfast: 11am

2 sips ginger ale (10 calories?)
2 cups green tea
1 bite soy green tea pudding (20 calories?)
Crispy brown rice cereal (100 calories?)
¾ cup of Rice Dream (90 calories)

### Lunch: 2pm

3 sips ginger ale (20 calories?)
¾ cup brown rice with hijiki, white beans, and greens
(300 calories?)
creamy tahini dressing (80 calories?)
¼ piece kabocha squash (15 calories?)

### Snack: 6pm

¼ peach (30 calories?)
1 cup Soy Delicious chocolate ice cream (250 calories)

**Dinner: 10pm**

Chicken soup with rice noodles (400 calories?)

¼ cup cottage cheese w/ pineapple (120 calories)

3 raspberries (4 calories)

cranwater (20 calories?)

**total caloric intake:** approx 1,459 calories

**Notes:** I FEEL LIKE TOTAL SHIT. A stomach thing and general fluishness. No appetite. But I am still doing great with my food attitude! Should have had more veggies and less sugar/carbs.

## THURSDAY AUGUST 26, 2010

**Late night snack: 4am**

¾ container of Fage 2% Greek Yogurt (110 calories)

raspberries (20 calories)

**Breakfast: 6:30am**

Gluten free honey oat toast (120 calories)

w/ almond butter (100 calories)

**9:30 am**

30 raspberries (35 calories?)

**1:45 pm**

weird orange juice/tracking liquid for cat scan (100 calories?)

**3 pm**

5 Raisinets (38 calories)

**5:30 pm**

¼ turkey on rye bread w/ lettuce and mustard (300 calories?)
2 bottles Teas green tea

**9 pm**

¼ small container *saag paneer* and white rice (380 calories?)
½ container chocolate soy delicious ice cream (230 calories)
green tea
seltzer

**Total caloric intake:** approx 1,433

**Notes:** Spent day in ER. Diagnosed with acute colitis. (Not the chronic kind! Maybe from the laxative tea?) Lots to say about that and I'll type it when not on jury duty. By which I mean Percocet. I meant Percocet and typed "jury duty." I think I overestimate my calories sometimes.

## FRIDAY, AUGUST 27, 2010

**Breakfast: 10:30 am**

2 bites Indian Ras Malai (100 calories?)
¾ gluten-free BBQ chicken pizza w/ added arugula (320 calories)

**4 pm**

rest of Indian Ras Malai (300 calories?)

**8 pm**

½ unripe peach (30 calories?)
1 piece gluten free honey oat toast (120 calories)
¼ bowl rice in soup w/ mushroom and umeboshi (250 calories?)

**12:30am**

¼ vegan chocolate chip cookie (65 calories)
2 scoops vegan cookie dough (280 calories)
¼ cup rice dream (60 calories)
gluten free cheerios (70 calories)

**total caloric intake:** approx 1,595

**Notes:** I am on antibiotics, no booze till I finish on Friday, September 10. Ran into Elaine and she noticed I'd lost weight. She thought it was illness but I know the truth of the matter. This feels like the healthiest and most sustainable eating pattern I've ever been in!

## SATURDAY, AUGUST 28, 2010

**11 am**

2 ¼ rolls of yuba skin (150 calories?)
¼ cup gluten free cereal (70 calories)
¼ cup rice dream (60 calories)

**12:30 pm**

¼ Granny Smith apple (40 calories)

**1 pm**

¼ roast turkey on rye w/lettuce and mustard (250 calories?)

**4:30 pm**

large almond butter, rice milk, fig smoothie (500 calories?)

**9:30 pm**

watercress salad w/crispy soy beans (60 calories?)
cabbage salad (20 calories?)
broccoli (40 calories?)
steamed greens (20 calories?)
creamy tahini dressing (90 calories?)
sesame dressing (40 calories?)
2 pieces prosciutto (70 calories)

**total caloric intake:** approx 1,410

**Notes:** I did some cocaine this evening! Joaquin showed up at the bar and I said I couldn't drink so he was like "do this cocaine." Just a bump. Then we went to another bar for hamburgers and I was angry and got in a cab. But I'm still feeling good about food—not emotional—and was getting mega compliments on my look at the bar. Still coming up short in the fruits/veggies arena. Tomorrow I'll start the day with a reasonable serving of yogurt and some dates, then have a lunch and dinner both full to bursting with veggies—that's what this body needs.

### SUNDAY, AUGUST 29, 2010

**2 am**

azuki bean mousse (250 calories)

**12 pm**

apple pie (450 calories)
bio-k (45 calories)
maple syrup (25 calories)

**1:30pm**

apple waldorf salad (350 calories)
¼ roast chicken breast (150 calories)
bite of cornbread (50 calories)

**4 pm**

small piece of milk chocolate (50 calories)
carrot/orange juice (120 calories)

**5pm**

small tasti d (80 calories)
large tasti d (150 calories)

**6 pm**

a bunch of lemon cake (300 calories)

**7 pm**

white wine (100 calories)

**8 pm**

steak, veggies (300 calories)

**10 pm**

more lemon cake (300 calories)
even more lemon cake (300 calories)
cereal and almond milk (250 calories)
banana (120 calories)
apple (85 calories)
¼ jar peanut butter (700 calories)

**total caloric intake:** 4,225 calories

**Notes:** I went totally nuts and ate all the things.

# *Sex Scenes, Nude Scenes, and Publicly Sharing Your Body*

MY MOTHER INVENTED the selfie.

Sure, there were self-portraits before her, but she perfected the art of the vulnerable candid with an unclear purpose. She used a Nikon, a film camera with a timer, and she would set it up, stand against the cherry-print wallpaper in her bedroom, and pose.

It was the early seventies. She had moved to the city armed with nothing but this camera and a desire to make work. She had left her boyfriend behind, a kindly balding carpenter from Roscoe, New York, who wore a flannel nightgown and knew how to tap trees for syrup. I happen to know he's kindly because we visited him once and sat around his table drinking lemonade, and he didn't seem mad that she'd left him, just happy for her successes and generally pleased about my existence.

When she got to New York she moved into the loft I'd grow up in, a little too big for a single girl and a little too small for a family. She took odd jobs to pay the rent—styling food and selling billiard balls and once, just once, taking a Japanese businessman on a tour of New York City nightlife. (A unique quality of my mother's is that when she's uncomfortable she expresses her purest and most deeply felt rage, so I'm guessing he had a bad time.)

In the images she took of herself in the loft, she was only sometimes dressed, in a baggy sweater or belted safari shorts. But most of the time she was naked. At least partially. Jeans and no shirt, her pale shoulders hunched, her knees knocking. A round-collared blouse and thick wool socks but no pants, the shadowy place between her ass cheeks revealed when she pulled knees to chin.

Over time, her hair changed: long ironed sheets became an ill-advised perm. A bob, the ends still wet from the shower. Her armpits tended to be unshaven, a look I regret knowing that my father enjoys. Sometimes she added a potted plant to the image for texture, like a student filmmaker creating a makeshift set of Vietnam.

On occasion she turned the lens toward the mirror so her face was obscured by the chunky black camera body, pulling focus to her dry heart-shaped lips and rabbit teeth (the same ones I have, the same ones she has since capped). But mostly, the eye is drawn to her nakedness. Legs spread defiantly. This wasn't officially her art, but she was committed.

The fact that she was shooting on actual film—and not an iPhone or a Polaroid bought at Urban Outfitters, à la the selfies of today—lent an appealing seriousness to her fascination with herself. Something about the intentionality of the medium. After all, she had to load the camera, print the film by hand in her darkroom, then hang the images on the line to dry. When her roommate Jimmy, a more seasoned photographer, wasn't around to ask for help, she called the Kodak hotline, which was manned by one single put-upon gentleman ("It's boiling hot in my darkroom and I've been putting ice cubes in my developer. Do you think that's okay?"). Embarrassed by the frequency of her calls, she would affect extreme accents to mask her voice. Imagine going to all that effort, just to find out what your bush looks like when paired with lime-green rain boots and shining aviators. This wasn't as simple as swinging your iPhone around and pushing your tits together. This took work.

My mother is slim. A long torso, loose arms, and a collarbone sheer as a rock face. But the camera clung to her imperfections—the ripple of fat below her butt, the sharp knob of her knee, the massive birthmark on her forearm that she had removed as a fortieth-birthday present to herself. I think of her developing these images, sloshing them around in the photo solution with a pair of salad tongs. Waiting, as they blushed gray, then appeared in full contrast, to see what she really looked like.

She convinced her little sister to pose, too. Her little sister: a blond med student with the kind of body designed to sprawl in wet sand. This feather-haired, horseback-riding beauty queen was suddenly sullen when her shirt was off. Shy. The camera, that great equalizer.

My mother understood, implicitly, the power of it. See these hips, these teeth, these eyebrows, these stockings that bunch and sag at the ankles? They're worth capturing, holding on to forever. I'll never be this young again. Or this lonely. Or this hairy. Come one, come all, to my private show.

When my father appeared on the scene there would be pictures of him, too, sitting in the bathtub, holding a frying pan up as a shield. As disconcerting as it is to see your father make a face that can only be described as "coquettish," it's the images of my mother that fascinate me. The flash of fear in her eye—or is it longing? The feverish need to reveal who she really is, as much to herself as anybody.

I get naked on TV. A lot.

It started in college. Pressed for actors who embodied the spirit of sexual despair I was looking to cultivate, I cast myself. Unaware how sex scenes were handled by the pros, I didn't purchase nudity covers or enforce a "closed set." I simply pulled my shirt over my head and dove in.

"Do you want me to actually suck your nipple?" Jeff, my confused scene partner, asked.

Later, looking at the footage in the Oberlin media lab, I didn't feel shy. I didn't love what I saw, but I didn't hate it either. My body was simply a tool to tell the story. It was hardly me at all, but rather a granny-panty-clad prop I had judiciously employed. I didn't look elegant, beautiful, or skilled. This was sex as I knew it.

Exhibitionism wasn't new to me. I'd always had an interest in nudity, one I would describe as more sociological than sexual. Who got to be naked, and why? The summer between fourth and fifth grades, I remember riding bikes with my best friend Willy around the lake in Connecticut where our families congregated for the summer each year—think *Dirty Dancing,* but with more known pedophiles in the neighborhood—when I became keenly aware that I was wearing a shirt and he was not. That didn't seem fair. After all, my mother had recently told me it was technically legal for women to walk through Manhattan shirtless, even if very few exercised the right. Why did Willy get to enjoy the summer breeze on his chest? What was so bad about exposing mine? I stopped, removed my t-shirt, and we pedaled on in silence.

In 2010 I got the opportunity to make a television show. The network told me they wanted to see my age group, the concerns of my friends and enemies, in graphic detail—and they didn't seem to be bluffing. If I was going to write honestly about twenty-something life, sex was a topic I'd have to address head-on. And the sex in television and movies had always rubbed me the wrong way. Everything I saw as a child, from *90210* to *The Bridges of Madison County,* had led me to believe that sex was a cringey, warmly lit event where two smooth-skinned, gooey-eyed losers achieved mutual orgasm by breathing on each other's faces. The first time I got naked with a guy, grotesque as it was, I was just so relieved he wasn't deeply inhaling my natural scent or running his hands up my torso to the strains of Chris Isaak.

Besides being gross, these images of sex can also be destructive. Between porn and studio romantic comedies, we get the message loud and clear that we are doing it all wrong. Our bedsheets aren't right. Our moves aren't right. Our bodies aren't right.

So when I was offered the chance to make the show, I did what I'd been doing for almost five years in far more "independent" productions: I stripped down and went for it.

People are always curious, so I'm going to tell you what it's like to lie in bed in a room full of onlookers and simulate inter-

course with someone you may or may not know. Professional actors always give canned answers like "It's just a job, it's so mechanical" or "He was so fun to work with, he felt like my brother," but since no one has ever accused me of being professional, *or* of being an actor—I will be honest.

It's fucking weird. Yes, it's just a job, *but* most people's jobs don't consist of slamming your vagina against the flaccid, nylon-wrapped penis of a guy wearing massive amounts of foundation to conceal his assne. I've suffered humiliations such as kneeing my scene partner in the balls, realizing under the bright studio lights that there is a thick black hair growing out of my nipple, and finding a lubricated prop condom stuck between my butt cheeks seven hours after arriving home.

It's hard to imagine that anything you do in a room full of lights, old Italian dudes, and bad tuna sandwiches is going to be seen on TV by multitudes, so I don't really think about the audience during my sex scenes. Getting naked feels better some days than others. (Good: when you are vaguely tan. Bad: when you have diarrhea.) But I do it because my boss tells me to. And my boss is me. When you're naked, it's nice to be in control.

And my mother always knew that, hence her Nikon raised high and pointed right into the mirror. She sensed that by documenting her own body, she was preserving her history. Beautifully. Nakedly. Imperfectly. Her private experiment made way for my public one.

Another frequently asked question is how I am "brave" enough to reveal my body on-screen. The subtext there is definitely how am I brave enough to reveal my *imperfect* body, since I doubt Blake Lively would be subject to the same line of inquiry. I am forced to engage in regular conversation about my body with strangers, such as the drunken frat boy on MacDougal Street who shouted, "Your tits look like my sister's!" My answer is: It's not brave to do something that doesn't scare you. I'd be brave to skydive. To visit a leper colony. To argue a case in the United States Supreme Court or to go to a CrossFit gym. Performing in sex scenes that I direct, exposing a flash of my weird puffy nipple, those things don't fall into my zone of terror.

A few years ago, after I screened *Tiny Furniture* for the first time, I was standing outside the theater in Austin when a teenage boy approached me. He was tiny. Really tiny. The kind of tiny that, as a teenage boy, must be painful. He looked like a Persian cat's toy mouse.

"Excuse me," he said shyly. "I just wanted you to know how much it meant to me to see you show your body in that way. It made me feel so much better about myself."

The first result of this was that I pictured him naked, which was stressful. The second was extreme gratitude: for his generosity in sharing, for my ability to have any impact on the body image of this obviously cool and open young gentle-man (after all, he was seeing a fringe women's-interest film on a school night).

"Thank you so much." I beamed. "You're really hot."

# *15 Things I've Learned from My Mother*

**1.** Luxury is nice, but creativity is nicer. Hence the game where you go into the ten-dollar store and pick out an outfit you might wear to the Oscars (or to the sixth-grade dance).

**2.** The sidewalk isn't really that dirty.

**3.** Barbie's disfigured. It's fine to play with her just as long as you keep that in mind.

**4.** If you have a bad feeling about someone, don't worry about offending them. Just run. Being polite is how you get your purse stolen or your "purse stolen."

**5.** Related: if someone says "I'm not going to hurt you" or "I'm not a creep," they probably are. Noncreeps don't feel the need to say it all the time.

**6.** Never yell at someone else's child. Just talk shit about them behind their back.

**7.** It's okay to ignore the dress code if you're an "artist." People will think you're operating on a higher plane and feel suddenly self-conscious.

**8.** If someone doesn't answer your email within six hours, it means they hate you.

**9.** "Asshole" is not a curse word. Not even if you add "little fucking" in front of it.

**10.** It's better to eat little bits of everything than large amounts of one thing. If that fails, try large amounts of everything.

**11.** Respect isn't something you command through intimidation and intellectual bullying. It's something you build through a long life of treating people how you want to be treated and focusing on your mission.

**12.** Keep your friends close. Buy your enemies something cool.

**13.** Why spend $200 once a week on therapy when you can spend $150 once a year on a psychic?

**14.** "Sometimes a dog smells another dog's tushy, and it just doesn't like what it smells."

**15.** Family first. Work second. Revenge third.

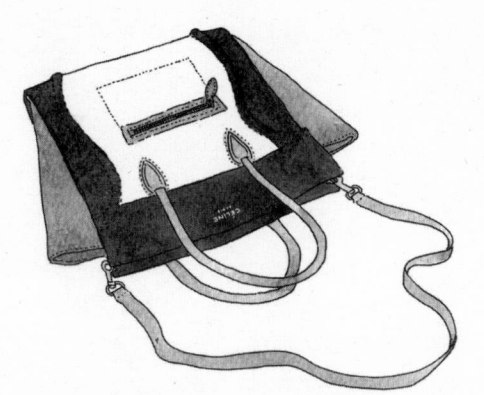

# *What's in My Bag*

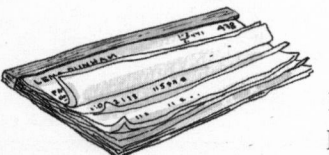

**1.** A stained, tattered checkbook. Because you just never know.

**2.** My new iPhone, along with my old broken iPhone, because I can't risk having someone find that iPhone who would know how to fix it and then see all the images I took of my own butt purely to educate myself.

**3.** An eyebrow pencil because I overtweezed my eyebrows like every child of the nineties and am now stuck with what my sister calls balding caterpillars. Weak eyebrows = weak presentation. It's like having a bad handshake,

but worse because it's right on your face.*

**4.** Advil, Lexapro, Mucinex, Klonopin, and Tamiflu, for emotional security. If you have any spare pills, I will take those, too, just to up the diversity of my portfolio. To be clear: I rarely take them. It's a knowledge-is-power situation. Sort of.

**5.** Business cards. For women as diverse as Ingrid the Muscle Whisperer and Sandra Fluke.

Once I was sitting in a Barnes and Noble café at 9:00 P.M., absorbed in a book about olive oil and waiting for a friend, when a business card appeared on the table. Handwritten, it said, "I just want to go down on you. I ask nothing in return. I will come to wherever you are. Please call me at: 212 555 5555." Later, dying of morbid curiosity, I pressed *67 and dialed. "Hello?" He sounded like Bruce Vilanch. I could practically sense his dying mother in the background. I ripped the card into tiny pieces, afraid of what might happen if I kept it in my possession. I so badly didn't want that guy to eat me out that it seemed destined to happen.

**6.** My building newsletter. The average age of our building's residents is eighty-five. The first night I slept in my apartment, I awoke at 7:00 A.M. to what can only be

---

* Since writing this, I have discovered dyeing my eyebrows, and life is approximately 63 percent better.

described as cackling. From my corner window, I could see three or four elderly women on the roof (enough to constitute a coven) wearing white hand towels on their heads and safari hats atop the hand towels, running through a choreographed routine.

The only neighbor close in age to me is a nine-year-old

named Elyse. Hoping to be a writer/baker someday, she took it upon herself to start the first building newsletter. There, she details holiday events, stoop sales, and the status of ongoing elevator repairs. She highlights exceptional neighbors. (UN translators! Opera singers!) Her prose is minimal and breezy, her layout festive. My only critique is that she's not settling into a regular publication schedule.

Elyse was not responsible for the memo about how to properly dispose of adult diapers that circulated last March.

**7.** My wallet. I bought my wallet while high off my ass on legal prescription drugs in the Hamburg airport. It is decorated with clowns, cars, and dachshunds and is uniformly beloved by children and Japanese women alike.

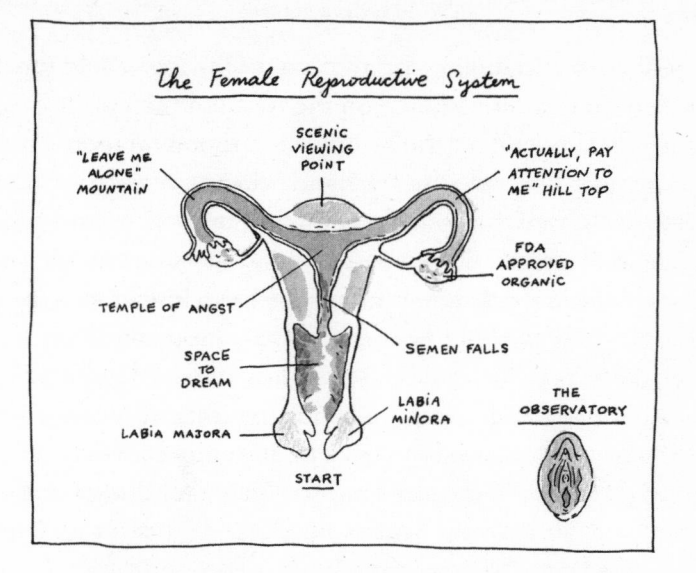

The Female Reproductive System

"LEAVE ME ALONE" MOUNTAIN

SCENIC VIEWING POINT

"ACTUALLY, PAY ATTENTION TO ME" HILL TOP

FDA APPROVED ORGANIC

TEMPLE OF ANGST

SPACE TO DREAM

SEMEN FALLS

LABIA MAJORA

LABIA MINORA

THE OBSERVATORY

START

# *Who Moved My Uterus?*

I'VE ALWAYS KNOWN there was something wrong with my uterus.

It was just a feeling, really. A sense that things were not quite *right* down there. The entire system. At a young age, four or five, I would often approach my mother with a complaint of stinging "in my area." Her cure-all was Vaseline, which she applied with a scientific distance. "Remember to wipe well," she reminded me. But I swore that wasn't it. I appreciated that she never used embarrassing pet names when it came to my private parts, unlike some other girls whose mothers say "pinky" or "chachi." In middle school, as my body prepared to menstruate for the first time, I could feel an electric current, an energy that felt wrong, intersecting lines of pain traveling through my pelvis and lower abdomen.

I got my period for the first time the summer before ninth grade, and that fall I took a dance class with my friend Sophie, whose mother was French and therefore encouraged ballet as exercise. Every Tuesday we would take the train to Park Slope to spend ninety minutes with an instructor named Yvette, whose mane of *Flashdance* hair, bell-sleeved shirts, and chipper demeanor could not mask how disappointed she was to still be doing this in her late thirties. In a windowless studio with scuffed wooden floors and a crooked Merce Cunningham poster, we learned modern ballet routines, running back and forth to the strains of "Nine to Five" and "Daydream Believer."

"I can't go," I told Sophie one Tuesday. "I have my period."

"A period isn't a reason to cancel something," she said, annoyed. "You just do everything you would usually do, but *with* your period."

But to me, it felt like the onset of the flu. A dull but constant backache. A need to bend and crumple at the waist for comfort. And an itchy sting, like an encounter with bad leaves, in my vagina and ass. How could anyone do anything when they felt this way? And would this really happen every month until I was *fifty*? My mother was fifty, and her nightstand was stacked with books with titles like *A Woman's Cycle* 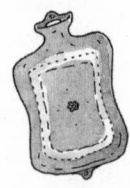 and *Second Puberty*. I asked her if she'd ever had cramps like mine. "Nope," she told me. "My period didn't give me any problems at all until it went away." Now she had to take all kinds of pills, use creams. I had recently found a medication of hers whose instructions said, "Insert pill vaginally at least five hours before a bath."

It didn't happen every month, as it turned out. Some months it happened. For days on end, it happened. Other times, it would seem like it was gone, and then I would wake up and think I had been shot in the crotch. The months it didn't happen at all never concerned me until I became sexually active and started keeping pregnancy tests in my sock drawer.

When I was sixteen I went to the gynecologist for the first time. They tell you that you can wait until you're either eighteen or sexually active, and I was neither, but I needed help. My period—the pain, the volatility, the feeling of utter despair—was taking my family hostage. And if my father asked whether I was possibly menstruating I screamed in his face so loud his glasses shook. Despite my virgin status the gynecologist prescribed birth control, which has helped with regularity, but nothing can help the mood that still descends a few days before my period begins, like a black cloud rolling in. I am uncharacteristically dark and nihilistic. Everyone is out to get me, to hurt me, to uninvite me from their tea parties, to judge my body and destroy my family. I am like a character on *Dallas,* obsessed with subterfuge and revenge, convinced I have discovered unlikely yet real-seeming plots against me. Once, while in the throes of PMS, I became convinced a man in a black overcoat was following me down La Cienega Boulevard. "The police will never believe me," I sighed, and began hatching a plan for losing him on my own.

When menstruating, I am the definition of inconsolable. *Cannot be consoled.* My friend Jenni swears my eyes take on a catlike slant and my face grows pale. If someone suggests it's hormonal, they are met with a deluge of verbal abuse, followed by aggressive apologies and pleas for forgiveness. Tears. I lie facedown and wait for it to pass.

Menstruating is the only part of being female I have ever disliked. Everything else feels like a unique and covetable privilege, but this? When it began, it held a morbid fascination, like a car crash that happened inside my underpants every three weeks. I was happy to be admitted into this exclusive club, to finally regard the tampon machine with the knowledge of the initiated. But it soon became tiresome, like a melodramatic friend or play rehearsals. There's something so demoralizing about the predictability of it all: We want chocolate. We are angry. Our stomachs puff out like pastries. Early on, I made a promise to myself never to use menstruation as a comic crutch or a narrative device in my work. Never to commiserate in a group about which pills actually take care of cramps. Never to say anything but "I have a stomachache." And I do.

Last summer my vagina started to sting. I would wake up more conscious of my genitals than usual and, as I came to, I'd realize why. As work began, as we all waved hello and ate our eggs on a roll and decided who to hate that day, I would feel it. It was like someone had poured a drop of vinegar inside of me, followed by a sprinkle of baking soda. It bubbled and fizzed and went where it would. I chugged water, having decided acidic urine was the problem. I took pills found in the refrigerated section at Whole Foods that my hairdresser suggested. I asked the doctor to test my urine and questioned the lack of results. I imagined the worst: a flesh-eating bacteria acquired in India making its way up my urethra, soon to turn me into a bag of bones. A tiny tumor, like a pea, sitting high up inside me. An imperceptible scratch from a sandy tampon.

I have a lot of worst nightmares, and chronic vaginal pain has long been among them. *The Camera My Mother Gave Me* is Susanna Kaysen's lyrical little memoir about her struggle with vaginismus, a pain in her vagina that she could neither explain nor ignore. I'm telling you: never have you read such a page-turner about female genitalia, and Kaysen masterfully illustrates the fact that the vagina is an organ uniquely qualified to express our emotions to us when we aren't capable of listening to our brains or hearts. And the vagina is our most emotional organ, subject to both science and spirit. At the height of her saga, Kaysen says:

"I wanted my vagina back. . . . I wanted the world to regain the other dimension that only the vagina can perceive. Because the vagina is the organ that looks to the future. The vagina is potential. It's not emptiness, it's possibility."

As a result of this book, I associate pain in the vagina with weakness and sadness. Kaysen has made a career out of turning her madness inside out for the world to see, and the book never does pin her vaginal pain on a single medical cause. Rather, she finds relief by exiting a bad relationship, reclaiming her life and spirit and, in the process, her vagina. So what  could I be suppressing that was filling me up with pain? Was it ambivalence about sex? Was I ever molested? (If so, that would explain some other things, too.) Was I afraid of where my career might be taking me, and was I running so far ahead of myself that I couldn't catch up? Did

I even know the difference between my urethra and my vagina?

The pain came and went, but my anxiety about it grew steadily. I avoided the doctor, sure the prognosis would simply be "basket case." But eventually my catastrophic thinking became unbearable, and my incredibly patient boyfriend became sick of the refrain "My vagina hurts." So I went to see Randy.

Randy is my gynecologist. I have had a number of gynecologists over the years, all talented in their own ways, but Randy is the best. He is an older Jewish man who, before deciding to inspect ladies down there for a living, played for the Mets. He still has the can-do determination of a pitcher on an underdog team and, to my mind, that is exactly the kind of man you want delivering your babies or rooting around in your vagina.

Which is exactly what he did one Thursday, as he asked me about work and told me about his son's new French bulldog. "Does it hurt when you schtup?" he asked. I nodded yes. He inserted the speculum as he described his wife's commitment to her spin classes. He said "I'm not a foodie" at least three times.

"Well, it all *feels* okay to me," he said. With the exception of a small bump of inexplicable scar tissue, my vaginal canal was just great. "But let's just take a closer look to be sure." He summoned the ultrasound tech, Michelle, who kept her engagement ring on her tanned, lumpy finger as she snapped a rubber glove on and covered the ultrasound wand with what appeared to be a dime-store prophylactic.

"Is that a condom?" I asked.

"Yeah, basically," she said.

"But is it different than a condom? Like, what do you call the product?"

"A condom."

Kind but firm, she slid the ultrasound wand inside me and watched the screen closely as she moved it back and forth. Randy watched with interest as Michelle attempted to part my large intestine like a curtain.

"Her uterus," she said. "Look. It's pretty far to the right."

Randy nodded. "But her ovary?"

"It's pinned against the wall."

"My uterus?" I asked.

"It's far over there," Randy said.

"There's some adenomyosis right there," Michelle said, pointing to a roiling gray shape. "But nothing larger than that. No cysts. The left ovary is—"

"No, it's the right ovary that's wonky," Randy said, taking the wand from her like an impatient kid playing a video game with a friend.

After a long moment, he patted my leg reassuringly and removed the wand in one swift motion. "Okay, hop up and get dressed and meet me in my office."

When they left, the sting was so bad that I shook my legs out, like a kid doing the hokey pokey, trying to redistribute the pain. When that didn't work, I bundled the blue cotton gown up and pressed it to my crotch like I was trying to stop up a wound.

In Randy's office, which is home to two mismatched regency chairs, a charcoal drawing of a pregnant woman, and a pair of decorative boxing gloves, he explained that I had classic endometriosis. Using a laminated picture from approximately 1987, he explained that endometriosis is when the cells that line the uterus are found outside the uterus, rising and swelling with the monthly hormonal cycle and causing many of the symptoms I had always considered to be my unique dysfunction, a sign that I wasn't strong enough for this world. The bladder pain, the stinging sensation, the ache in my lower back, were all the result of growths the size of pinheads that were dotting my once-pristine organs. He couldn't say for sure without surgery, but he'd seen enough of these cases to feel fairly confident. And the adenomyosis— when the endometrial cells begin growing into the muscles surrounding the uterus—was a telltale sign. In the drawing Randy showed me, it looked like hundreds of seed pearls working their way into soft pink velvet. He was kind enough to also show me some photographs he had taken during laparoscopic surgeries, of cases worse than my own. The photos looked like the remains of a wedding: rice scattered, cake smushed. A little bit of blood.

"Does this explain why I'm so tired?" I asked, hopeful.

"I mean, if you're in pain half the month, then yeah, you're gonna be tired," he agreed.

"And would this, like, affect my fertility?" I asked tentatively.

"It can make it harder to get pregnant," Randy said. "It doesn't mean it will. But it can."

·  ⌐●  ·

"Do we all have uteruses?" I asked my mother when I was seven.

"Yes," she told me. "We're born with them, and with all our eggs, but they start out very small. And they aren't ready to make babies until we're older." I looked at my sister, now a slim, tough one-year-old, and at her tiny belly. I imagined her eggs inside her, like the sack of spider eggs in *Charlotte's Web*, and her uterus, the size of a thimble.

"Does her vagina look like mine?"

"I guess so," my mother said. "Just smaller."

One day, as I sat in our driveway in Long Island playing with blocks and buckets, my curiosity got the best of me. Grace was sitting up, babbling and smiling, and I leaned down between her legs and carefully spread open her vagina. She didn't resist, and when I saw what was inside I shrieked.

My mother came running. "Mama, Mama! Grace has something in there!"

My mother didn't bother asking why I had opened Grace's vagina. This was within the spectrum of things that I did. She just got on her knees and looked for herself. It quickly became apparent that Grace had stuffed six or seven pebbles in there. My mother removed them patiently while Grace cackled, thrilled that her prank had been such a success.

For as long as I can remember, I have wanted to be a mother. In early childhood, it was so extreme that I could often be found breastfeeding stuffed animals. When my sister was born, family legend has it that I asked my mother if we could reverse roles: "Let's tell her I'm her mother and you're her sister. She won't ever know!"

Over time, my belief in many things has wavered: marriage, the afterlife, Woody Allen. But never motherhood. It's for me. I just know it. Sometimes I lie in bed next to my sleeping boyfriend and puff out my stomach, imagine that he is protecting me and I am protecting our child. Sometimes we talk about how exciting it would be if something happened accidentally, if we were faced with becoming parents without having to make the decision ourselves. I name them in my head, picture picking them up in the park, hauling them through the Gristedes when we all have colds, stopping by a picnic "just for five minutes because he's really sleepy." Reading *Eloise* to my three-year-old daughter for the first time. Running around and shutting the windows before a storm, explaining: "This will keep us nice and dry!"

When I tell my doctor aunt about my endometriosis diagnosis ("endo" for those in the know), she says I better get cracking. "In medical school, that was the first thing we were taught," she says. "After an endo diagnosis you say *get started now.*"

My doctor never said that to me. He was casual—now that I consider it, too casual? I had been right all along, known better than any doctor: something really *was* wrong down there.

So I have to get started now. It's time to get started now. And why not? I wonder. I have a job. I am in love. We have an extra bedroom that we are currently using for shoes, boxes, and occasional guests. I am told my dog is unusually good with children. I already look fucking pregnant. Why *the hell* not?

I can feel them. The babies. They're not crawling all over me. They're not vomiting in my hair or shrieking. They're doing perfectly normal baby things, and I'm keeping them alive. But I resent them. Their constancy, their intrusion on my relationship and my free time and my naps and my imagination and my heart. They've come too soon, and I can't do any of what I had planned. All I can do is survive.

My most frequently recurring dream is one in which I suddenly remember I have a number of pets living in my home that I haven't tended to in years. Rabbits, hamsters, iguanas, stacked in dirty cages in my closet or beneath the bed. Terrified, I open the door, and the light touches them for the first time in ages. Desperate, I dig through the clumped, wet wood chips. I'm afraid they're decomposing in there, but I find them still alive, thin and milky eyed and filthy. I know that I loved them once, that they had a better life before I got so distracted with work and myself and let them shrivel up and nearly die. "I'm sorry, I'm so sorry," I tell them as I clean their cages and fill their bottles with fresh water. "How can I make it up to you?"

# SECTION III
# *Friendship*

# *Girl Crush*

*That Time I Was Almost a Lesbian, Then Vomited*

*You wrote me a beautiful letter,—I wonder if you meant it to be
as beautiful as it was.—I think you did; for somehow I know
that your feeling for me, however slight it is, is of the nature of
love. . . . When you tell me to come, I will come, by the next
train, just as I am.*

**—Letter from EDNA ST. VINCENT MILLAY
to EDITH WYNNE MATTHISON**

I'VE HAD EXACTLY ONE serious girl crush, a term I have
been taught to hate by women I admire (but do not, in fact,
have girl crushes on). Also, being in possession of a gay sister,
I find the term "girl crush" slightly homophobic, as if I need
to make it clear that my crush on another woman is not at all
sexual but, rather, mild and adorable, much like . . . a girl.

My crush's name was An Chu. I was in third grade, she in fourth. She wore thermal t-shirts, wide-leg jeans, and a headband on her hairline, creating the impression that it was holding on a glossy black wig.

She was, in hindsight, maybe gay—into kickball, the kind of swagger that isn't designed to arouse guys but does anyway during the preboner years when a girl being able to horse around is a bigger sexual stimulant than boobs. A laser-sharp focus on her select group of girlfriends. An was gorgeous like a lady but unknowable like a man. She was active but quiet. Her smile was slow, and her head was too big for her body, and when I looked at her I felt uncomfortably warm.

We never spoke, but I watched her closely on an overnight class trip to a nature retreat, gazed as she shook a rain stick and analyzed an owl pellet, and after my parents picked me up early (I had barfed), I spent the next weekend in the guest room at my grandma's house imagining An and me sharing secrets in the dim orange light of a sleepover.

I haven't had a crush on a woman since, unless you count my confusing relationship with Shane from *The L Word*. I've never wanted to be with women so much as I wanted to *be* them: there are women whose career arc excites me, whose ease of expression is impressive, whose mastery of party banter has me simultaneously hostile and rapt. I'm not jealous in traditional ways—of boyfriends or babies or bank accounts—but I do covet other women's styles of being.

There are two types of women in particular who inspire my envy. The first is an ebullient one, happily engaged from morning until night, able to enjoy things like group lunches, spontaneous vacations to Cartagena with gangs of girlfriends, and planning other people's baby showers. The bigger existential questions don't seem to plague her, and she can clean her stove without ever once thinking, What's the point? It just gets dirty again anyway and then we die. Why don't I just stick my head . . .

My grandma Dottie is this kind of woman. At ninety-five, she still gets her hair done twice weekly, is always armed with a tube of coral lipstick, and offers advice for the lovelorn ("You have to be positive and just talk with your eyes"). She's been teeny tiny her entire life, and once, at a military dance in the late '30s, a soldier told her, "I could eat peanuts off your head," which she took as a massive compliment.

The modern version of this is my friend Deb, who loves trying new exercise classes and is able to write for the same four hours every day in the same coffee shop, unconflicted about the creative process. She had a revolving door of casual dinner dates when she was single, before she met her husband and fell in love with him, never once accusing him of not understanding "what it feels like to be me." Deb plans regular weekend getaways to "sexy, delightful" places like Palm Springs and Tulum and is a master at the logistics of dinner parties and doctor's visits. She doesn't seem to worry that she has lupus or cancer. It would be easy for me to jealously dismiss Deb as flighty or superficial, unaware of what's *really* going on in the world. But Deb's smart and, I told you, I am jealous.

The other type of woman that gets me crazy with envy is the beautiful depressive. I know it's not good to glamorize depression, but I am speaking here of a more low-grade melancholy that would be a massive bummer in your supermarket checkout guy but works pretty well for a certain kind of long-limbed, lank-haired aspiring actress-poet. One Sunday I was walking around Brooklyn, looking for rice pudding, when I ran into the girlfriend of a close male friend of mine. She was jogging, milky legs extending for miles from her retro track shorts.

"How are you doing, Leanne?" I asked.

She looked at me all sleepy eyed and, with a Victorian sigh, said: "Shitty." I was so impressed! Who answers that question honestly? Let's say I was on my way to buy a gun with which to kill myself and I ran into a casual acquaintance who works in PR for H&M:

CASUAL ACQUAINTANCE: Hey, what's up?
LENA: Oh, not much. Just going to buy something weird. [*Giggles.*]
CASUAL ACQUAINTANCE: Long time, no see. How ya been?
LENA: Oh, ya know. *Así así!* Life is such a WEIRD thing, ya know? It's like OFF THE WALL! I mean, we should get coffee sometime. I'm literally free anytime.

As I watched Leanne slo-mo jog home, I thought of how effective that routine must be. Leanne is so beautiful and sad. Her boyfriend will spend years going on midnight errands for her, just trying to make her smile. I used to think guys liked it when you're cheerful, adaptable, and quippy. In fact, pouting in front of a Nature Channel show and forcing them to wonder what you're thinking after sex is, in most cases, far more effective.

I have been envious of male characteristics, if not the men themselves. I'm jealous of the ease with which they seem to inhabit their professional pursuits: the lack of apologizing, of bending over backward to make sure the people around them are comfortable with what they're trying to do. The fact that they are so often free of the people-pleasing instincts I have considered to be a curse of my female existence. I have watched men order at dinner, ask for shitty wine and extra bread with a confidence I could never muster, and thought, What a treat that must be. But I also consider being female such a unique gift, such a sacred joy, in ways that run so deep I can't articulate them. It's a special kind of privilege to be born into the body you wanted, to embrace the essence of your gender even as you recognize what you are up against. Even as you seek to redefine it.

I know that when I am dying, looking back, it will be women that I regret having argued with, women I sought to impress, to understand, was tortured by. Women I wish to see again, to see them smile and laugh and say, *It was all as it should have been.*

In eighth grade, my class took a field trip to Washington, D.C. This is a tradition for eighth grades around the country, the premise being that you will see the monuments, learn about the various branches of government, and enjoy some well-deserved time at Johnny Rockets. The reality is that the day is just a way to get to the night, when the curtains are pulled back to reveal a circus of debauchery that every chaperone wisely chooses to "sleep" through. Students run from room to room of some airport Marriott, their wildest selves unleashed, screaming to be heard over the TVs and rap music and running showers with nobody in them. Sometimes there's booze in a shampoo bottle; sometimes people kiss in a bathroom.

It was on the second night of the trip, as we watched a Drew Barrymore movie on basic cable, that every girl in my suite—Jessica, Maggie, even Stephanie, who had a SERIOUS BOYFRIEND—decided to go totally gay. It started with some light kissing on the bed, then Jessica was topless and shaking her tits, clutching her own nipples and waggling them mercilessly in our faces.

I was a shelter dog, frozen with fear. It wasn't that I didn't want to join in. I sort of did. But what if I *liked* it? What if I started and I never stopped? How could I turn back? I had no issue with gay people. I just didn't want to *be* one. I was fourteen. I didn't want to be *anything* yet. I curled up and, like our math teacher in the room next door, pretended to sleep.

·  🫧  ·

I'd heard about Nellie—a prodigious British playwright whose Wikipedia page said she was two months younger than I. An actor I know had performed in Nellie's only New York production and described her as Tinker Bell or Annabel Lee—or Pattie Boyd right around when she was really fucking shit up for George Harrison. An intellectual with a penchant for deep emotional connection, drunken dancing, vintage coats slung over one shoulder.

Pictures of Nellie on the Internet revealed a pale waif with a mess of bleached hair and an outfit like a modern Joan of Arc, all pale rags and androgynous angles.

A Google search of Nellie's name was unsatisfying. She didn't have Twitter, a blog, or any other form of personal Internet expression. A scant web presence is so rare these days, alluring in and of itself. She was telling her story through the ancient medium of theater.

Months into my Google gumshoe work on Nellie, she appeared at a talk I was doing at the *New Yorker* festival. It was a hard crowd to make giggle, and they were full of self-serious questions about race and sexual politics that I answered unsteadily, tired and underprepared. Afterward I met Nellie in the green room and shook her frail hand and was surprised by how deep her voice was, like an old British man's. Her eyes were half closed, her collar buttoned up as high as it could go. She looked like Keats or Edie Sedgwick or some other important dead artist.

"I'm such a big fan of yours," I told her, having only ever Google-image-searched her. I had never read a word of her work, but, looking into her heart-shaped face, I wanted nothing more than to make a lasting impression. *Hi, I'm Lena,* I wanted her to feel, *and I like theater and stoops and parties where people cry.*

"Thank you, thank you," she purred.

When I was fifteen my friend Sofia taught me her favorite trick, one that she said drove the boys crazy. She presented it like it was a complex act that required expert instruction, but really it was just sucking someone's earlobe. She was ahead of me in the sex game, and I tried hard to act like this was something I'd gotten up to before.

It was late, and I could hear my parents' dinner party winding down, people gathering their coats, my father prematurely washing the dishes, his way of signaling that the night was over.

Sofia was explaining to me how stupid boys are, how a few tricks could bring them to their knees in a matter of seconds. She was wearing a tight white t-shirt and stonewashed jeans that cut into the meat of her waist. She had the kind of glossy hair that was always slipping out of its ponytail and permanently reddened skin.

She demonstrated on me, on the mattress in my "office"— actually a crawl space off my bedroom where we kept crafting supplies and the litter box. I could feel the tips of her teeth and then my pulse in my vagina.

I am going to London. All alone. I haven't been to London since age fourteen, when I was angry my mother forced me to ride a Ferris wheel and even angrier because I liked it.

Unsure of how to use this time, I decide to email Nellie, whose work I have now read and found as impressive and impenetrable as her person.

When Nellie replies, she calls me Darling Girl. I suggest tea, but she'd rather have a drink and says she'll "come round" to pick me up at five thirty. She emails to tell me she'll be late, then again to say that she's early. When I find her in the lobby, she's wearing slim leather pants and a long black coat. Her purse looks like a pirate's treasure sack.

Our first stop is the "social club" she belongs to, down the block and underground. A wood-paneled, dusty room, low ceilings, and cigarettes smoked inside. Nellie orders red wine, so I do, too, fiddling nervously with the strings of my purse. She introduces me to various Wilde-ish characters and mentions Aristotle, Ibsen, and George Michael in one breath (that last one is her neighbor). She orders us new glasses of wine before I'm done with my first, then realizes that we're late for our dinner reservation at J. Sheekey. She leads me through the West End by the hand, tells me this restaurant is where her parents would always take her if she'd made good grades or needed a talking-to. She tells me about secret affairs and secret passageways. She loves walking, does miles every day.

At J. Sheekey, a fancy old fish restaurant where they systematically ask whether you're trying to make it to a theater engagement before you sit down, she orders expertly, white wine and tiny fried fishes and other things I'm squeamish about eating, but when they come they are purely delicious, like butter or syrup. My face is getting warm, and I may already be sharing too much. I'm supposed to have drinks with friends in an hour, but she begs me to cancel and come back to her house. "It's an unusual place and I want you to meet everyone and everyone wants to meet you."

In the cab to her house, we talk. About why we write, what its purpose is when, she says, "the world is full of so much shit we can't fix."

"And in our work, we create a better or clearer universe," I tell her breathlessly. "Or at least one that makes more sense."

"A place we'd want to live, or can at least understand." She nods, satisfied. "You're really smart."

I realize I've never talked to anyone else about this, much less a woman my own age. I've never talked to anyone my own age about anything beyond ambition. Technique, passion, philosophy, we don't touch any of that.

She asks me my worst quality, and I say I can be very self-involved. She says hers is that she gets lost in the world of her work and can't find her way back out again.

The city is changing, from bustling metropolis to tree-lined streets and grand houses with only a few lights on. (Google "British lawns" if you want to know what I'm talking about.) When we reach her house we step out into the wet night. The cobblestones are hard to navigate in heels, and I cling to Nellie's arm. I am sure I've never been any place like this. It has the grandeur of a fairy tale and the grit of a Mike Leigh movie. I breathe in, wet street and distant smoke. I guess she paid for the cab.

She opens the door into a library that looks

like a set from an episode of *Masterpiece Theatre,* aged books scattered everywhere. They even spill out of a fireplace.

"Hello!?" she calls out. A deranged French bulldog bounds down the grand staircase, baring her teeth. "Oh, come on, Robbie."

A girl wearing animal ears hops out from a secret door. She greets me with a hug, and I follow them to a living room where four or five roommates congregate over a bottle of red wine. Each is introduced to me as an actor or a literature student or both. Her sister, another imp with impossibly well-thought-out hair, has a funny phlegmy laugh.

I know I shouldn't drink anymore, or should at least temper it with a few handfuls of the crisps they are passing around. No one can explain how they came to live here. Nellie hops up, discarding her coat while announcing that it's freezing. "Let me show you round," she says.

I take in every detail of the house like I'm six again and reading a picture book, scanning the illustrations carefully. Next to a marble fireplace lies an issue of *Elle,* a torn thigh-high stocking, an empty pack of Marlboros, a half-eaten pudding cup. And each room leads to another, like one of those

New York real-estate dreams where you open a hidden door and discover massive rooms you didn't even know you had. I spill some of my wine down the front of my dress.

Nellie's bedroom contains a free-standing claw-foot tub, and I eye all her books and clippings with a pathetic level of interest. Nellie says she spent all of yesterday in bed with an off-limits woman, recovering from a night that undid her. I tell her again how much I love her work, which I really do. She works with themes, memes, metaphors. Uses formal tricks beyond my grasp.

"Nobody our age writes like you," I tell her.

"Thank you, thank you," she says.

Back in the living room they've started blasting old-school rap, and my glass has been refilled. I can't sit without my skirt riding up. Jenna, a pretty girl known for playing Anne Frank on the West End, gives Nellie a fat kiss on the mouth and says, "Hello, I'm home." I feel most warmly toward Aidan, a former child actor of ambiguous sexuality who has the soft delivery of a boy working in a flower shop.

They are teaching me all sorts of new British terms—such as *lairy,* which means "rowdy" or "drunkenly mischievous," and they use it in all sorts of contexts for me: "I got pretty lairy after a few drinks and next thing I know I was hanging from the chandelier."

They refill my glass and then refill it again. We are laughing, laughing at faces and sounds and objects, then suddenly everything goes in waves, and my vision narrows in a way that can only mean vomit.

As soon as I announce it, it's happening. A torrent released on their heretofore intact cream carpet. I feel the hot, acidic remains of my dinner running down my chin and hitting the floor, and I'm too sick to be self-conscious. It's too much of a relief to care that every English treat I have eaten that day, along with glass upon glass of red wine, is now decorating their floor. Nellie pets my head, cooing endearments. I rear up, look around. Everyone is just where I left them except Aidan, who reappears with a broom and dustpan that he uses to sweep up my barf like it's packing peanuts or hair trimmings. He insists he does this all the time. I'm still not embarrassed.

Nellie moves in close to me.

"You have such a beautiful face," she tells me. "Such amazing eyes. You're so fit."

"Are you kidding?" I slur. "You're a perfect-looking creature. And so smart. And I feel . . . I feel like I understand you."

She holds my face, panting like we're out in a snowstorm. Her eyes grow huge, and without words I understand. She knows I understand what is missing. Someone is gone. She beats her chest with a tight fist. "But it hurts so much. You can't *believe* how much it hurts."

"I know," I tell her, and for that moment I do. "I know, I know. You're so brave."

She lies down next to me. We're face-to-face now. Jenna is dancing over us, laughing, having stripped down to only a sports bra.

"It's hard to talk about," she says. "I love knowing you."

I squeeze her. I feel as though I've never felt another person's pain more deeply. I imagine my breath is terrible, but I also imagine she doesn't mind things like that. And I don't mind when she blows smoke in my face. I rustle her hair, my own, hers again. I didn't think she'd kiss me, but I didn't think she wouldn't either. I said I was leaving an hour before I actually left, and in the cab home I clutched a piece of paper with her number on it and thought about how I hadn't gotten to see her pond.

The next morning, I sleep until almost 3:00 P.M., lulled by the sound of cabs pulling up to my hotel in the rain. I have meetings in the afternoon and am determined not to tell anyone I vomited. But sharing is my first instinct, and I offer it up ten minutes into my first professional engagement of the day. I nurse a single cup of tea until, around 6:00 P.M.,

I'm ready to eat the crust of a potpie. I pull out my phone and start scrolling through images of the night before, none of which I have a memory of taking. In one, Aidan menaces the camera, blurry. In another Jenna kisses my sweaty face. In a few Nellie's cigarette waves wildly, threatening to set fire to her house. In others we are face-to-face, eyes closed. Our hands are clasped.

If you look carefully you can see, in the upper-left-hand corner, the purple specter of my vomit.

· *0* ·

I kissed three girls in college. All at once. Three straight girls were experimenting with universal love in a corner at a party to benefit Palestinian rights and, when they offered me membership, I took it. We went around in a circle, taking turns, kissing for just long enough to get a sense of one another's mouths. They felt soft and tickly to me, minus the hard edges and rough bits I was still getting used to on boys. Afterward we laughed. None of my eighth-grade fears had come true. I was not, suddenly, the militant lesbian leader of a motorcycle gang, nor was I ashamed. I didn't even flinch when a photo of me, mid-lip-lock, with a girl named Helen surfaced in the art building, part of a boy named Cody's "Nan Goldin–inspired thesis."

· 1 ·

Later, alone in bed and almost over the nausea of my hangover, I zoom in on the picture of Nellie and me. The uncropped version, that is. Conspiratorial, sickly, lost girls on a good sofa. If I were a slightly different person, I'd have had many nights like this, a hard drive full of these images. I may hate the term "girl crush," but a picture does not lie. It has the quality of an image taken by a ghost hunter, revealing floaters and spirits that the participants had been unable to see.

## The Best Part

"I DON'T THINK this is working out," he says. "I think we would be better off as friends."

It's seventh grade, and we've just come back from winter break. On our last date we walked up and down the street holding hands for a few hours before going into Häagen-Dazs to wait for my mom to pick me up. I know I like him because when his teeth filled with seeds from a Very Berry Smoothie it didn't gross me out at all. Next Wednesday would have been our six-month anniversary.

"Okay," I squeak before throwing myself into the bosom of Maggie Fields's blue fur coat. She smells like cotton candy, and she feels so sorry for me, leading me into the girls' bathroom on the twelfth floor and petting my head. He was my first boyfriend, and I feel sure I'll never have another. Maggie has had three, and all of them disappointed her.

"What a dick!" she says. "What are we gonna do to him?" Her Brooklyn accent only comes out when she's angry. This is the best part.

·  ·

"I can't do this anymore," I say, and crumple against the window.

He sits in the driver's seat of his green jeep, wondering what I'm so upset about while I cry behind my sunglasses. We park in silence, and he leads me back to his apartment like I'm a little kid in trouble. We shut the door, and he fills a Mason jar with water and tells me I'm the only person who has ever mattered to him. He says he knows I feel the same way, his face contorted in the only display of emotion I've seen since we met.

Finally, after three more attempts at ending it—at the beach, on the phone, via email—I sit with my friend Merritt at a sidewalk café in Park Slope. It's a little too cold to be outside and we wear our sunglasses, shrinking down into our hoodies. I pick at my pancakes while she tells me, simply, "It's okay to change your mind." About a feeling, a person, a promise of love. I can't stay just to avoid contradicting myself. I don't have to watch him cry.

So I stop answering the phone, I stop asking permission, and soon he's completely gone, like being grounded over Christmas break or some other terrible thing that seemed like it would last forever.

"When you're my age, you'll know how mysterious this all is," he says.

He's talking about love, and he's only eight years older than me. I should have known. It was going almost too well, a bicoastal relationship. He called me every morning on his way to the beach to surf. I described the view from the window of my new apartment, snow falling on the neighbor's garden, local cats whining from their respective fire escapes. I couldn't always remember his face, so my visual for him became my feet, bare and pale and pressed against the wall as we talked for hours. "I wish you were here," he said. "I'd take you for ice cream and show you the waves."

I nodded. "I'd like that." Or I'd like to like that.

But here I am at his birthday party, all wrong in my mother's black dress, face red, braid greasy, heels sinking into the soil of his friend Wayne's backyard. The girl who is DJing has eleven buns in her hair, and he is standing by the hot tub talking to another girl in a romper, and I know, as much as I have ever known anything, that my arrival isn't what he'd imagined. Maybe he never really imagined it at all. The next day he takes me on a day trip up the coast that should be romantic but feels like a hostage situation. As we wait in line for fish tacos, I hope against hope that no one can hear him speaking, and if they do, they don't judge me for it. I want more than anything to be alone.

I head home, and having concluded this chapter I am able to relax for the first time in months. After all, desire is the enemy of contentment. From the bathtub, I call Audrey. "It isn't going to work," I tell her. "I think he thinks he was being really deep by dating a chubby girl." Later, we will find out he was simultaneously courting an actress from television's *The West Wing* and that he bought her a cactus.

Audrey starts to laugh. "What a goon. He's lucky to know you, but too stupid to ever realize it."

· ❧ ·

"I still love you," he says, "but I have to go my own way."

"So you want to break up?" I ask, trembling.

"I guess so," he says. I fall to the floor, like a woman in the twelfth century fainting at the sight of a hanging in her town square.

Later, my mother comes home from a party and finds me catatonic, lying across the bed, surrounded by pictures of him and me, the mittens he bought me at Christmas folded beneath my cheek. I am crippled by what feels like sadness but what I will later diagnose as embarrassment. She tells me this is a great excuse: to take time for myself, to cry a bunch, to eat only carbohydrates slathered in cheese.

"You will find," she says, "that there's a certain grace to having your heart broken." I will use this line many times in the years to come, giving it as a gift to anyone who needs it.

# 13 Things I've Learned Are Not Okay to Say to Friends

**1.** "She's chubby in a different way than we are."

**2.** "Don't worry, no one will remember this when you're dead."

**3.** "No, please don't apologize. If I had your mother I'd be a nightmare, too."

**4.** "It's all right. Honesty has never really been your thing."

**5.** "Maybe you should open a store? That would be a good job for you!"

**6.** "Holocaust, eating disorder. Same difference."

**7.** "I Googled him and 'rape' autofills after his name."

**8.** "But it's different because I actually *have* a dad."

**9.** "Come on, please let me pay for lunch. You don't have a job!"

**10.** "There's a chapter about you in my book."

**11.** "There's nothing about you in my book."

**12.** "Oh, hey, your boyfriend tried to kiss me while you were off getting a smoothie. I mean, either that or he was smelling my mouth."

**13.** "Have a nice life, bitch."

# *Grace*

I WAS AN ONLY CHILD until I turned six.

I figured, knowing what little I did about reproduction and family planning, that this was how it was always going to be. I had heard the kids at preschool discussing their siblings or lack thereof:

"My mommy can't have another baby."

"My daddy says I'm *just* enough."

"Do you have brothers or sisters?" my teacher asked me on the first day of preschool.

"No," I replied. "But my mommy is pregnant with a baby."

She wasn't pregnant with a baby, not even a tiny bit, and had to explain as much when the teacher promptly congratulated her on the "coming addition."

"Do you want a brother or sister?" my mother asked me

that night as we ate takeout Chinese off the coffee table. "Is
that why you lied?"

"Sure," I responded, as casually as if she'd offered me an
extra moo shu pancake.

So, unbeknownst to me, my vote tipped the scales, and
they began to try in earnest. I continued with my routine,
unaware of the storm brewing in the bedroom down the hall.
And two years later, on a boiling day in June, my mother
turned toward me from the driver's seat of our Volvo and
said, "Guess what? You're going to have a baby sister."

"No, I'm not," I replied.

"Yes, you are," she said, smiling wide. "Just like you wanted."

"Oh," I told her. "I changed my mind."

Grace came late in January, on a school night, no less. My
mother's water broke, splashing the hardwood in front of the
elevator, after which she waddled back to my bedroom and
put me to sleep. When I woke up at 3:00 A.M. the house was
dark, save for a light glowing from my parents' bedroom. I
crept down the hall, where I found a babysitter named Be-
linda reading on their bed, next to a porcelain doll I had re-
quested from an ad in *TV Guide* (five payments of $11.99)
and a pile of wrapped peppermints.

In the morning I was walked down Broadway to the hospital, where Grace was the only Caucasian infant in a nursery of
Chinese babies. I peered through the glass: "Which one is
she?" I asked.

My mother lay in a hospital bed. Her belly still looked as
full as it had the day before but soft now, like a Jell-O mold. I
tried not to stare at her reddened breasts, hanging from her
kimono. She was tired and pale, but she watched me expec-

tantly as I sat in a chair and my father placed the baby carefully in my lap. She was long, with a flat red face and a bulbous, flaky skull. She was limp and helpless, flexing and unfurling her minuscule fist. I found my new doll significantly cuter. He held up the Polaroid camera, and I raised Grace like I would the prize rabbit at a 4-H fair.

I spent Grace's first night at home wailing "INTRUDER! RETURN HER!" until I exhausted myself and fell asleep in an armchair. The feeling was so sharp, so distinctly tragic, that I have never forgotten it, even though I have never felt it again. Maybe it's the sensation of finding a lover in your spouse's bed. Maybe it's more like getting fired from the job you've had for thirty years. Maybe it's just the feeling of losing what is yours.

From the beginning, there was something unknowable about Grace. Self-possessed, opaque, she didn't cry like a typical baby or make her needs clear. She wasn't particularly cuddly, and when you hugged her (at least when *I* hugged her), she would wriggle to get free like a skittish cat. Once, when she was around two, she fell asleep on me in a hammock, and I sat as still as I could, desperate not to wake her. I nuzzled her downy hair, kissed her chubby cheek, ran my pointer finger along her thick eyebrow. When she finally awoke it was with a jolt, as if she had fallen asleep on a stranger on the subway.

Grace's playpen sat in the middle of the living room, between the couch and the dining room table I had carved my name into. We conducted our lives around her, my parents talking on twin telephones, me drawing pictures of "fashion girls" and "crazy men." Occasionally I would kneel on the floor in front of her, stick my face into the mesh of her enclosure, and coo, "Hiii, Graaacie." Once she leaned in and placed her lips on my nose. I could feel them, hard and thin, through the barrier. "Mom, she kissed me! Look, she kissed me!" I leaned in again, and she bit down hard on my nose with her two new teeth and laughed.

As she grew, I took to bribing her for her time and affection: one dollar in quarters if I could do her makeup like a "motorcycle chick." Three pieces of candy if I could kiss her on the lips for five seconds. Whatever she wanted to watch on TV if she would just "relax on me." Basically, anything a sexual predator might do to woo a small suburban girl I was trying. Maybe, I thought, she would be more willing to accept kisses if I wore the face mask my grandmother had for when she did her dialysis. (The answer was no.) What I really wanted, beyond affection, was to feel that she needed me, that she was helpless without her big sister leading her through the world. I took a perverse pleasure in delivering bad news to her—the death of our grandfather, a fire across the street—hoping that her fear would drive her into my arms, would make her trust me.

"If you don't try so hard it'll be better," my father said. So I hung back. But once she was sleeping, I would creep into her room and listen to her breathe: in, out, in, out, in again, until she rolled away.

· 🏸 ·

Grace always intrigued adults. For starters, she was smart. Her interests ranged from architecture to ornithology, and she approached things much more like an adult than with the irksome whimsy of a precocious child. As a little girl I had been obnoxiously self-aware, irritatingly smug, prone to reading the dictionary "for fun" and making pronouncements like "Papa, nobody my age enjoys real literature." Things I'd heard "special" people say in movies. Grace simply existed, full of wisdom and wonder, which is why we often found her in the bathroom at a restaurant, talking a forty-year-old woman through a breakup or asking what a cigarette tasted like. One day we found her in our pantry swigging from a small bottle of airplane vodka, disgusted but intrigued.

On only one occasion did her maturity go too far. It was the dawn of social media, and Grace, then in fifth grade, asked me to make her a Friendster account. Together we listed her interests (science, Mongolia, rock 'n' roll) and what she was looking for (friends) and uploaded a blurry picture of her blowing a kiss at the camera, clad in a neon one-piece.

One night I picked up my computer, and it was open to Grace's Friendster messages. There were a dozen or so, all from a guy named Kent: "If you love Rem Koolhaas, we should definitely meet up."

Always the alarmist, I woke up my mother, who confronted Grace about it over whole-wheat pancakes the next morning. Livid, Grace refused to speak to me for several days. She didn't care whether I was trying to protect her, or what "Kent" the "ad sales rep" had in mind. All that mattered was that I had told her secret.

·  🐌  ·

In college, my dormmate Jessica started dating a girl. To me, it seemed sudden and rash, a response to trendy political correctness rather than basic human desire. "She's trying to prove she's not just another JAP," I told people. "She broke up with her boyfriend like two weeks ago! All she cares about are shoes and dresses."

Her girlfriend, a pretty-faced soft butch with round glasses and hunk-at-the-sock-hop hair, had graduated already and would drive to Ohio every other weekend, at which point I would have to clear out, sleeping on the floor of someone else's room, so they could go down on each other for infinity.

Sometimes I would ask her to tell me about the sex and whether someone else's vagina was insanely gross.

"No," she said. "I actually like doing it." "It" meant "oral sex."

Grace came to visit me at school one weekend, and I brought her to a party. By this time she was fifteen, all legs and eyes and fawn-colored freckles, with shiny brown hair that fell down her back and two-hundred-dollar jeans she had somehow convinced my father she needed. She stood in the corner, laughing and nursing the single beer I had promised her.

Oberlin being a liberal haven where opposition was king, the coolest clique at school was a group of rugby-playing, neon-wearing lesbians. They dominated every party with their Kate Bush–heavy mix tapes, abstract facepaint, and pansexual energy. "Kissing is a dance move," their leader, Daphne, once explained to me.

And that night Daphne noticed Grace, her little puppy nose and the big ridged teeth she still hadn't grown into, and dragged her onto the dance floor.

"We're alive!" she shouted, and Grace was embarrassed, but she danced. Awkwardly at first, then with conviction, engaged but not overly eager. I watched her from the sofa with pride. *That's my girl. She can roll with anything.*

"Your sister's gay," my Jessica announced the next day, folding the fresh laundry spread across her twin bed.

"Excuse me?" I asked.

"I'm just saying, she's into girls," she said casually, like she was offering me a helpful tip on how to save money on car insurance.

And I completely lost it: "No, she's not! Just because you're gay for a *second* doesn't mean everyone else is too, okay!? And not that I'd care if she was, but *if* she was, I would know. I'm her sister, okay? I'd know. I know everything."

Grace came out to me when she was seventeen. We were sitting at the dining room table eating pad thai, our parents out of town, as they often were now that we were old enough to fend for ourselves. Twenty-three and sponging mightily, I forked some noodles into my mouth as Grace described a terrible date with a "dorky" boy from an uptown school.

"He's too tall," she moaned. "And *nice*. And he was trying too hard to be witty. He put a napkin on his hand and said, 'Look, I have a *hand cape*.'" She paused. "And he draws cartoons. And he has *diabetes*."

"He sounds awesome!" I said. And then, before I considered it: "What are you, gay?"

"Actually, yes," she said, with a laugh, maintaining the composure that has been her trademark since birth.

I began to sob. Not because I didn't want her to be gay—in truth, it worked perfectly with my embarrassing image of myself as the quirkiest girl on the block, hence my recurring suggestion that my parents foster a child from a third world background. No, I was crying because I was suddenly flooded with an understanding of how little I really knew:

about her pains, her secrets, the fantasies that played in her head when she lay in bed at night. Her inner life.

She had always felt opaque to me, a beautiful unibrowed mystery just beyond our family's grasp. I had been telling my parents, sister, grandma—anyone who would listen, really—about my desires from an early age. I live in a world that is almost compulsively free of secrets.

When Grace was three, she came home from preschool and announced she was in love with a girl. "Her name is Madison Lane," she said. "And we're going to get married."

"You can't," I said. "Because she's a girl."

Grace shrugged. "Well, we are."

Later, this became a favorite family story: the year Grace was gay, the Madison Lane incident. She laughed, as if we were telling any silly baby story. *We* laughed like it was a joke.

But it wasn't a joke. And Grace's admission felt not like a revelation but a confirmation of something we all understood but refused to say. Throughout high school Grace remained above the fray. She was president of speech and debate, attending a rhetoric match, then running off to tennis lessons in a crisp white skirt, skeptical of the hormonal hysteria that had overtaken her girlfriends. She's too mature, we thought, too *unusual* to get caught up in crushes. We said, "College will be her time. For satisfaction, for relaxation, for boys."

Grace was polite, firm, and unemotional as she answered my questions, continuing to eat her pad thai steadily and check her phone every few minutes. The basics: When did you know? Are you scared? Do you like someone? Then the ones I couldn't ask: *What have I ever said that let you down, that failed you or made you feel alone? Who did you tell before you told me? Is this my fault because of the dialysis mask?*

She said she'd already had a romance, a girl named June

who was her roommate on a summer program in Florence. They kissed most nights and, she said, they "never really talked about it." I tried to imagine June, but all I could picture was a snowy-white mannequin in a wig.

My discomfort with secrets made waiting for Grace to come out to my parents torturous. I begged her to tell them, saying it was for her sake but knowing it was for my own. Sitting with the knowledge, the divide it created in our home, was too much for me. I had never been comfortable with what was not said, and there was nothing I would not say. But Grace wasn't ready, despite my cajoling and kicking her under the dinner table. I held my tongue, despite my fear that I would have a Tourette's moment and shout, *Grace is gay!*

One morning, my mother emerged from her bedroom, eyes sunken, hair askew, bathrobe still on. "I didn't sleep at all," she said wearily. "Grace has a secret, I know it."

I gulped. "What do you think it is?"

"She stays late after school, she ignores me when I ask her questions about her day. She seems distracted. I think"—she took a pained sip of her coffee—"I think she's having an affair with her Latin teacher."

"Mom, *no*," I said.

"Well, how else do you explain it?"

"Just think," I hissed. *"Think."* I waited, though not long enough, for her to understand. "Grace is gay!"

She cried harder than I had, like a surprised child. Or like a mother who had gotten something wrong.

A few years after she came out, Grace admitted that the June encounters were a fiction. She had invented them as a means of proving to anyone who questioned her that she was really gay. I was relieved to learn she hadn't fallen in love without telling me.

Grace is graduating from college. The four years since she left home have lessened her mystery and deepened her sense of self. She's emerged as a surprising, strange adult, still prone to bouts of moody distance but also possessed of a high cackle and a desire to have constant and aggressive fun. Sometimes she hugs and tickles me, and her long, cold fingers annoy me, a reversal of fortune I never imagined possible. When she writes, which isn't often, I get insanely jealous of the way her mind works, the fact that she seems to create for her own pleasure and not to make herself known.

She dresses like a Hawaiian criminal, loose, patterned shirts and oddly fitting suits, loafers without socks. Her attitude toward sex is more modern than mine and has a radical element I chased but never found. She wakes up with her hair knotted and leaves the house like that, often not returning home until late. She has a taste for unusual women, with strong noses and doll eyes and creative dispositions. She has a strong sense of social justice and an eye for anachronisms and contradictions. She is thin but physically lazy. Guys love her.

I LiKE YOUR CiTY...
I JUST LiKE MiNE
BETTER.

# *10 Reasons I <3 NY*

**1.** Because everything is everyone's business, but every story starts with "There I was, minding my own business . . ."

**2.** Because the rules are really more like suggestions.

**3.** Because it's more than just Manhattan, or even Brooklyn. Places like Roosevelt Island and City Island and Rikers Island! Did you know that there is a commune on Staten Island that has a dwarf chef? Did you know that there is a Colonial mansion in Brooklyn where a Japanese surgeon lives with his blind wife, or so I was told? Did you know that you can buy a tiny turtle with highly contagious salmonella in Chinatown that is so adorable you will want to risk it?

**4.** I have a passion for cabdrivers. I forever stand by the statement that there is no more brilliant, diverse, eccentric group of human beings on this planet than the men (and rare women) employed by the Taxi & Limousine Commission of New York. My father drove a cab for six months in the late seventies, and I told everyone in the second grade it was still his job.

**5.** Because everyone hates a suit. Even the suits.

**6.** Because if I see another film that's a "love letter to New York" or in which "New York is really the third character in this romance," I'm going to explode with rage, and yet I still recognize that nothing looks better on camera than a Midtown corner in winter or the Staten Island Ferry in high August.

**7.** Because of the twenty-four-hour pharmacy on Forty-eighth and Eighth, where a 3:00 A.M. plea for a Klonopin refill is treated like buying milk at 5:00 P.M. in Bethesda.

**8.** Because the people may not be polite, but when it counts they're something better than polite: they're kind. They're always letting you take your tea when you're short on change. Or letting you take the first cab if you're crying. Or letting you pee when you didn't even buy something. Or rushing to your side when you step in a pothole wearing platforms and eat it, hard. Helping you trap the lop-eared, terrified rabbit that has been living in a Dumbo parking lot for weeks. Giving you directions home.

**9.** Because everyone gets catcalled. And I mean *everyone*. If you have a vagina, by birth or by choice, you will be called *"mami"* or "sweetie" or "Britney Spears." And the catcalls can be so creative! Once, my little sister was walking down the street in her thick black glasses, and a homeless man muttered, "Talk nerdy to me."

**10.** Because I was born here, and New York is no alien: she is in my gut like an old sickness. Sometimes I'll be walking in Soho or Brooklyn Heights, and a smell, some brand of stale air, stops me dead in my tracks. Bound up in that smell: what it felt like to be dragged home from Balducci's on a hot night with a blister from my jelly shoe, begging every step of the way for a cab, realizing with horror that I was so close to my house I could see it and still I was on foot. The shady view from the window of my dentist's waiting room, before she stuffed her fat fingers in my mouth. The day we were so late to school and it was raining so hard that we caught a ride in the back of a soy-milk truck, which my mother denies to this day. Sitting in an alley with some guys from a different school, watching them smoke. Waiting for my parents to get home because I'd lost my keys and pissing in someone's potted plant. Looking down and realizing I am inexplicably up to my knees in mud. The time I took a cab on my birthday and it hit an old woman, and she lay in the street, teeth knocked out, while the cabdriver held her bloody head in his arms, and I shrunk down low until finally a pedestrian tasked with moving the car out of the intersection noticed me cowering, and I gasped, "It's my birthday." The time I was in a sundress walking my dog and locked eyes with a guy on a bicycle, and he rode right into a parked car and I ran. Each corner is a memory. In that way, it's just like every town.

# SECTION IV
## *Work*

# This Is Supposed to Be Fun?
*Making the Most of Your Education*

NOBODY BELIEVES THIS STORY.

It was the spring of third grade; our class was taking an overnight trip to a camp called Nature's Classroom, where we would spend three days learning about teamwork, ecology, and history in a remote corner of upstate New York. I had been sick about it since the moment I found out, two months before, and brought the permission slip home to my parents secretly hoping they would hand it back to me and say, *No way! No daughter of ours is going to the woods for three days! FORGET ABOUT IT.*

I didn't have friends. Whether this was by choice or not was a question I seemed unable to answer, for myself or for my parents, who were obviously concerned. I was anxious simply leaving my family for the day and made a collect call to my mother every lunch period, my stomach tightening when I couldn't reach her. The best news I ever could have received would have been that my parents had decided to homeschool me, to remove all pretense of socialization and just let me spend my days with them in their studios, where I belonged.

Really, I'd hated school since the day I got there. My father often repeats the story of my initial reaction to kindergarten: I came home from the first day and plopped down at my pint-sized desk.

"So, how'd it go?" my father asked.

"It was fun," I said. "But I don't think I'll go back."

He gently explained that wasn't an option, that school is to children as work is to grown-ups: it's what you do. And so I would have to go every day, rain or shine, with only occasional exceptions for illness, until I turned eighteen. "Then," he said, "you can decide what to do next." That was thirteen years away. I couldn't imagine thirteen more minutes of this, much less thirteen years.

But there I was, having made it to third grade, headed upstate in a fifteen-passenger van while Amanda Dilauro showed me a sheaf of pictures of her cat Shadow. The first thing I did when we reached our bunk was drop my backpack on the vinyl mattress and vomit.

Over the next few days, we were led from activity to activity. We played tambourines, weighed our leftovers before adding them to the compost pile, pretended eggs were our precious babies and carried them around our necks in padded cups dangling from twine. And then, on the final day, it was time for the faux Underground Railroad.

This is the part that no one believes.

"No adult would ever do that," they say. "You can't be remembering that right."

I am, in fact, remembering it perfectly. The counselors "shackled" us together with jump ropes so we were "like slave families" and then released us into the woods. We were given a map with a route to "freedom" in "the North," which must have been only three or four hundred feet but felt like much more. Then a counselor on horseback followed ten minutes later, acting as a bounty hunter. Hearing hooves, I crouched behind a rock with Jason Baujelais and Sari Brooker, begging them to be quiet so we weren't caught and "whipped." I was too young, self-involved, and dissociated to wonder what kind of impact this had on my black classmates. All I knew was that I was miserable. We heard the sound of hooves growing closer and Max Kitnick's light asthma wheezes from behind an oak tree. "Shut *up*," Jason hissed, and I knew we were cooked. When the counselor appeared, Sari started to cry.

Back at base camp, the counselor who became a bounty hunter became a counselor again and explained how many Americans traveled the Underground Railroad and how many didn't survive it. As he spoke, he pulled out a cardboard timeline of the Civil War, and all I could think was: This is stupid. This is so *so* stupid.

What were we going to learn from being lashed together with our classmates and chased by a pony? Would we suddenly empathize, be able to fully imagine the experience of the American slave?

A month after Nature's Classroom, my slave brother Jason Baujelais was suspended for casual use of the N-word. The exercise was a failure.

Fifth grade was when you made the switch to middle school, and with it came new privileges: elective classes and pizza Fridays and free periods in the library. My fourth-grade classroom was across the hall from fifth-grade history, and sometimes that teacher, Nathan, left his door open so we could hear him explaining Mesopotamia to a group of laughing eleven-year-olds. I'd seen Nathan around. He was the definition of gangly. His hair was thinning, and he cut the sartorial figure of Bob Saget, but he was youthful in the way he bounded around the classroom, using silly voices like Dana Carvey's, my favorite, and holding contests to see who could say "like" the least. The fifth-graders all said he was the best.

One day, our fourth-grade hamster, Nina, had babies. Six of them. They looked like chewed-up tomatoes, which is what I told our teacher when I summoned her to the cage. "I think she barfed fruit or something."

Kids crowded around the cage, but by the afternoon they had lost interest. I, meanwhile, became obsessed, particularly with the runt, which was black and white and about the size of a fava bean. I named it Pepper. As Pepper grew, it became clear there was an issue: its back legs were fused together by some kind of membrane that looked like pink bubble gum stretched thin. As a result of this deformity it had to drag itself around by its front legs, and it usually got left behind. Kathy, our teacher, was concerned: soon Pepper might get beaten to the food bowl, bullied, or worse. Nathan, she told me, was a hamster expert. He had fifteen of them at home. Perhaps I could take Pepper across the hall and see what he had to say.

I approached cautiously at lunch, carrying Pepper in an open shoe box. I paused at the door, watched him for a moment at his desk hunched over a sandwich, a juice box, and a grown-up novel. "Hello?"

Nathan looked up. "Hello."

I explained the situation in fits and

starts, trying simultaneously to convey the gravity of Pepper's case and take in the reality of a *fifth-grade classroom*. He motioned for me to hand him the box. He peered in, picking Pepper up in a confident motion, holding her under the tiny armpits while he examined the lower extremities. He removed a pair of nail scissors from his desk drawer, and I watched him cut Pepper's legs apart. "It's a she," he said. She was mewing, kicking her newly freed feet. "She'll be fine."

·  ♀  ·

The next year, when I got to Nathan's class, I felt like I already knew him. He acted like he knew me, too. And he noticed: that I loved to read and write and act and also that I had no friends. He invited me to stay with him for lunch, so I didn't have to stand out in the courtyard with everyone I hated, huddling in the corner to stay warm while sportier types sweated and had to remove their overlayers. We would usually end up talking: about books, rodents, the things that scared me. He told me his wife had died right after his daughter was born and that he had gotten a new wife, but he didn't like her as much. He said it was hard to find someone you wanted to spend that much time with. His energy shifted: some days he was calm and funny. Others he was antsy and tense, stopping every few minutes to shoot Nasonex up his left nostril. "Stupid allergies."

I'd never had a teacher talk to me this way. Like I was a person, whose ideas and feelings mattered. He wasn't just nice. He saw me for who I felt I was: achingly brilliant, misunderstood, full of novellas and poems and well-timed jokes. He told me that popular kids never grow up to be interesting and that interesting kids are never popular. For the first time, I looked forward to school. To the moment I'd walk into the classroom and catch his eye and feel certain I was going to be heard that day.

He called me "My Lena," which became Malena. At a certain point he started rubbing my neck while he talked to the class. He put a heart on the board every time I said "like," but just a check for the other students. I was terrified of what the other kids would think and thrilled to have been chosen. One day he brought his daughter to class, and she sat on his lap during lunch, drinking a juice box, her feet dangling, skimming the floor. She looked just like him in a wig. I wanted to kill her.

That winter, Jason Baujelais (now seemingly forgiven for the N-word incident) announced he hadn't done his homework. "Well, that's a problem," Nathan said, arms crossed.

"You never make Lena do her homework," Jason said.

I froze. Nathan approached slowly and asked me to open my backpack. I unzipped it, terrified of what might fall out. There were piles of unfinished worksheets, half-finished papers, all of which he had just stopped asking me for. He said he'd rather read my stories.

"You better have all this done by tomorrow," he told me.

I had picked up a dollar bill that had fallen out of my bag, and I was feeling it, turning it over in my sweaty hand. He snatched it.

"You can get this after class."

Once the classroom emptied out, I approached him. "Hi. Can I have my dollar?"

He smiled and stuck it down his shirt.

"Okay, now I don't want it." I giggled, hoping it would calm us both down.

He chucked it at me. "Jesus, Lena. You're all talk, but when it comes to action . . ."

It would be years before I knew what he meant, but I knew

I didn't like the sound of it, and I told my mother, who looked like she had seen a parade of ghosts. "That fucking pervert," she said, furiously dialing my father. "Come home from the studio now."

The next morning, she marched into school with me rather than dropping me on the steps. I waited outside the principal's office, catching snippets of my mom's muddled but distinctly angry voice. I stared at the linoleum floor, wondering whether I was in trouble. After a while, she stormed out, grabbing my hand. "We're getting the fuck out of here."

Fifteen years later, I met a man whose daughter was in Nathan's class, at a different school in a different borough.

"Oh, you should watch it," I told him matter-of-factly, trying to sound more relaxed than I felt. "He was inappropriate with me."

His face turned stormy. "That's a pretty big accusation."

"I know," I said, rushing to the bathroom before he could see me cry. I was reminded again that there are so many things we need that can also hurt us: cars, knives, grown-ups. I was reminded how no one really listens to kids.

I switched schools in seventh grade, to an institution whose values aligned with my own, and for six years school was as okay as it would ever be. I wrote poems, sprawling epics with curse words and casual mentions of suicide that didn't get me sent to the school psychologist. (I'm not sure there was a school psychologist.) We put on plays, some of them about lesbians or cat breeders or both. Our teachers engaged us in lively debate and were willing to say "I don't know" when they didn't know. I was allowed to circulate literature about veganism in the stairwell. A teacher and I had a misunderstanding and we "talked it out." It didn't feel inappropriate. It felt real.

I was not a perfect student—far from it. I was overmedicated and exhausted, wearing pajamas and a vintage hat with a veil. I struggled to stay awake in art history class. I had an authority problem. But I was living in a world where we were understood and honored for what we had to offer. I was allowed to take my puppy to gym class. My best friend played a didgeridoo he bought off the Internet. It was a best-case scenario for a worst-case problem: the fact that the government says we have to go to school. And when it was finally time to leave, I wasn't ready.

I bounded into Oberlin, thrilled to have been accepted and ready to learn with a capital *L*. I was keen on becoming a creative writing all-star and had prepared a "portfolio" of my poems and short stories for the head of the department. Dressed in bookish cords, I waited outside her door during office hours to discuss it with her.

"Well," she said. "You clearly write a lot."

"Oh, thank you! I do," I told her. "Every day!" Chipper, as if she'd given me a massive compliment and not just stated a fact.

"There are some interesting moments, but you don't have a particular facility for any genre. The poems feel like stories. The stories feel like plays."

I nodded, like, *great point.* "Yes! I also write plays."

"And the story," she said, "about the fake Underground Railroad. That just feels like satire, like something from *The Onion*. It's a bit broad, obvious."

All I could muster was a tiny "But it really happened to me."

She nodded, clearly unimpressed.

She let me in, but with reservations, and my rage from this tiny encounter fueled me and I became the most combative girl in every writer's workshop. The one who crossed out sentences dramatically in front of the writer of the piece. The one who posited the ever-so-helpful "What if ALL of this is bullshit?" I had begged my way in, and now I wanted out. But first I wanted everyone to realize what they were doing to us, these teachers. Draining us of our perspective, teaching us to write like the poets they admired—or, even worse, like them. There were only three teachers I liked. One because he seemed to have other interests, another because he smoked and cursed, and a third because his ex-wife wrote a memoir about him cheating on her with a French teacher that sold fairly well. He was now with another, different French teacher and wore a diamond earring, appearing unfazed.

·◇·

My parents have authority problems. In second grade, my mother was sent home from school for trying to organize a protest in which every girl defied the dress code and wore pants. She found her teachers not only boring but repulsive, especially the ones who were trying to embrace the counter-culture. They couldn't trick her with their long center-parted hair, their amber beads, their use of the word "vibe." Even now, a part-time teacher herself, she is horrified by the idea of anyone telling her what to think or do. She is also opposed to socializing with her students, mortified that anyone would think she was pulling the "cool teacher" move. "There is nothing more disgusting than being the oldest lady at the party," she likes to say.

My father, meanwhile, began his academic career as the shining star of the Southbury, Connecticut, public school system. Class president, book-club leader, smiling bucktoothed in a necktie on the Student of the Month placard. But like all the men in his family, he was eventually shipped off to boarding school, and by the time he got to Andover he was fifteen, shaggy haired, and angry, refusing to attend chapel or even class. When I read *Catcher in the Rye* it was instantly familiar, like an extension of the stories my father would tell on a long car ride. My father's journey from emblem of academic excellence to deadbeat burnout was a classic narrative but a potent one. I felt pride imagining the moment he realized it was all bullshit, man, and at his bravery for refusing to be carried along with the current. One time he cut class and walked into the woods and out onto the surface of an icy pond, only to fall through into the freezing water. After a terrifying struggle, he caught hold of the ice and pulled himself out and ran, soaking, back to the safety of his dormitory. But his life had flashed before his eyes. He could have died. After all, nobody knew where he was.

*      *
·  *＊*  ·
          ●

I went through brief phases of being a good student. Showing up early to my seminar with a mug of tea, taking cogent notes with a mechanical pencil, carrying my books close to my chest like a girl in a movie about Radcliffe. I loved doing it right—the ease of it, the tidiness of my objectives, which were simply to understand and express that understanding.

But inevitably it faded. A month into the semester, I would start showing up twenty minutes late to class again, with a bag of Cheez Doodles and a cup of cold grits, having left my note-book at home. The rewards weren't enough to keep me on task, and life got in the way. My mind wandered to the future, postcollege, when I'd create my own schedule that served my need to eat a rich snack every five to fifteen minutes. As for the disappointment written across the teacher's face? I couldn't, and wouldn't, care.

I was fifteen minutes late to graduation. My mother forgot the peach silk dress I planned to wear, and so I bought a vintage sari and piled my hair atop my head and trooped out to the arch in the middle of Tappan Square and waited for the music to start. My boyfriend, already graduated, lay out on the lawn. My father wondered why he had worn a suit. We were given two options: walk around the Tappan Square arch if you don't support the imperialist missionaries who installed it or walk through it if you don't know, don't care. I can't remember which option I chose, only that I couldn't believe I had never noticed the pregnant oboist in line in front of me. As we strode onto the lawn, I nodded at the teachers, dressed to the nines in their Hogwarts garb for the tenth, thirtieth, fiftieth year in a row. *Later, motherfuckers.*

I go back to Oberlin in the dead of winter to give a "convocation speech" in Finney Chapel, the largest and most historic of campus structures. In a subconscious nod to my college experience I forget to pack both tights and underwear and have to spend the weekend going commando in a wool skirt and kneesocks. I am toured around the school like I'm a stranger by a girl who didn't even go here. We stop at a glossy new café for tea and scones. She asks if I want a tour of the dormitories—no, I just want to wander around alone and maybe cry.

That it's been six years since I graduated from college seems impossible. Older folks laugh at my naïveté, saying that six years is nothing in the scheme of life. But now I've been gone longer than I was there. Soon, my life as a student will be as far behind me as summer camp.

I head down to the basement of Burton Hall where they've assembled a question-and-answer session, with student journalists sitting in a messy half circle around me. I make sure to keep my legs crossed, so as to avoid the headline: "Returning Alumna Flashes Vagina." Most of them ask sweet, neutral questions: "What do you think is the most beautiful spot in Oberlin?" "If you could take one class again, which would it be?" Others have a sharper edge and seem to be looking for the big scoop: "How does it feel to be a line item in so many people's narratives of privilege and oppression?"

I don't have a good answer. I look around for a sympathetic face before muttering, "There are some worse guys than me."

One student warns me that there is a protest planned outside my lecture tonight, though she can't seem to explain exactly what it's about. It reminds me of the time I joined a student walkout, got up and left history class, hoping all the way that someone would tell me where we were going and why.

That night, on the stage of Finney Chapel, I feel adrenalized and inchoate, like I have something to prove and no drive to do it. I've braided my hair and I can feel it sliding, slowly but surely, down my neck in wet clumps. A favorite professor asks me thoughtful questions, and I answer as best I can, with sound bites that have worked in the past.

"I feel like I have to bring up some of the controversy surrounding your work," he says.

"Okay, bring it up!" I'm trying to speak from a place of calm and strength, but it comes out more like a shriek. "Bring it up, and tell those protesters to come in, and we will talk like adults, not just freaks with signs! We will talk to each other and just WORK IT OUT! Because at the end of the day, we're all pissed about the same thing, you know? Having to be in school."

He looks at me blankly. The audience shifts, with discomfort or confusion or both. In an instant it becomes clear to me that there are no protesters, probably never were. If they planned something, they all bailed. There's just me, them. Us.

The next morning I leave at 8:00 A.M. Driving through town in the snow, I see my memories plainly. There I am in my long sleeping-bag coat, shuffling to class twenty minutes late on a Tuesday morning. There I am in what used to be the video store, piling my arms high with VHSs. There I am in the diner, ordering not one but two egg sandwiches. There I am in the gym, riding an Exercycle from the early '80s and reading a book called *Bosnian Rape*.

And there I am, drunk on a spring night, yanking my tampon out and hurling it into a bush outside the church. There I am falling in love by the bike rack. There I am slowly realizing my bike has gone missing from that same rack, stolen while I was sleeping. There I am calling my father from the steps of the art museum. There I am half listening to a professor when she tells me I need to start attending class more regularly. And I'm there, too, dragging a torn sofa into the black-box theater with my "set designer."

If I had known how much I would miss these sensations I might have experienced them differently, recognized their shabby glamour, respected the ticking clock that defined this entire experience. I would have put aside my resentment, dropped my defenses. I might have a basic understanding of European history or economics. More abstractly, I might feel I had truly *been* somewhere, open and porous and hungry to learn. Because being a student was an enviable identity and one I can only reclaim by attending community college late in life for a bookmaking class or something.

I've always had a talent for recognizing when I am in a moment worth being nostalgic for. When I was little, my mother would come home from a party, her hair cool from the wind, her perfume almost gone, and her lips a faded red, and she would coo at me: "You're still awake! Hiiii." And I'd think how beautiful she was and how I always wanted to remember her stepping out of the elevator in her pea-green wool coat, thirty-nine years old, just like that. Sixteen, lying on the dock at night with my camp boyfriend, taking tiny sips from a bottle of vodka. But school was so essentially repulsive to me, so characterized by a desire to be *done*. That's part of why it hurts so bad to see it again.

I didn't drink in the essence of the classroom. I didn't take legible notes or dance all night. I thought I would marry my boyfriend and grow old and sick of him. I thought I would keep my friends, and we'd make different, new memories. None of that happened. Better things happened. Then why am I so sad?

# Little Leather Gloves
*The Joy of Wasting Time*

*I remember when my schedule was as flexible as she is.*

—DRAKE

I WORKED AT THE BABY STORE for nine months.

Just recently graduated, I had stormed out of my restaurant job on a whim, causing my father to yell, "You can't just *do* that! What if you had children?"

"Well, thank God I don't!" I yelled right back.

At this point, I was living in a glorified closet at the back of my parents' loft, a room they had assigned me because they thought I would graduate and move out like a properly evolving person. The room had no windows, and so, in order to get a glimpse of daylight, I had to slide open the door to my sister's bright, airy room. "Go away," she would hiss.

I was unemployed. And while I had a roof over my head (my parents') and food to eat (also technically theirs), my days were shapeless, and the disappointment of the people who loved me (my parents) was palpable. I slept until noon, became defensive when asked about my plans for the future, and gained weight like it was a viable profession. I was becoming the kind of adult parents worry about producing.

I had been ambitious once. In college, all I seemed to do was found literary magazines with inexplicable names and stage experimental black-box theater and join teams (rugby, if only for a day or so). I was eager and hungry: for new art, for new friendship, for sex. Despite my ambivalence about academia, college was a wonderful gig, thousands of hours to tend to yourself like a garden. But now I was back to zero. No grades. No semesters. No CliffsNotes in case of emergency. I was lost.

It's not that I didn't have plans. Oh, I had plans. Just none that these small minds could understand. My first idea was to be the assistant to a private eye. I was always being accused of extreme nosiness, so why not turn this character flaw into cold hard cash? After hunting around on Craigslist, however, it soon became clear that most private eyes worked alone—or if they needed an assistant, they wanted someone with the kind of sensual looks to bait cheating husbands. The second idea was baker. After all, I love bread and all bread by-products. But no, that involved waking up at four every morning. And knowing how to bake. What about preschool art teacher? Turns out that involved more than just a passion for pasta necklaces. There would be no rom-com-ready job for me.

The only silver lining in my situation was that it allowed me to reconnect with my oldest friends, Isabel and Joana. We were all back in Tribeca, the same neighborhood where we had met in preschool. Isabel was finishing her sculpture degree, living with an aging pug named Hamlet who had once had his head run over by a truck and survived. Joana had just completed art school and was sporting the festive remains of a bleached mullet. I had broken up with the hippie boyfriend I considered my bridge to health and wholeness and was editing a "feature film" on my laptop. Isabel was living in her father's old studio, which she had decorated with found objects, standing racks of children's Halloween costumes, and a TV from 1997. When the three of us met there to catch up, Joana's nails painted like weed leaves and Monets, I felt at peace.

Isabel was employed at Peach and the Babke, a high-end children's clothing store in our neighborhood. Isabel is a true eccentric—not the self-conscious kind who collects feathers and snow globes but the kind whose passions and predilections are so genuinely out of sync with the world at large that she herself becomes an object of fascination. One day Isabel had strolled into the store on a dare to inquire about employment, essentially because it was the funniest thing she could imagine doing for a living. Wearing kneesocks and a man's shirt as a dress, she had been somewhat dismayed when she was offered a job on the spot. Joana joined her there a few weeks later, when the madness of the yearly sample sale required extra hands.

"It's a ball," said Isabel.

"I mean, it's awfully easy," said Joana.

Peach and the Babke sold baby clothes at such a high price

point that customers would often laugh out loud upon glimps-
ing a tag. Cashmere cardigans, ratty tutus, and fine-wale cords,
sized six months to eight years. This is where you came if you
wanted your daughter to look like a Dorothea Lange photo or
your son to resemble a jaunty old-time train conductor, all
oversize overalls and perky wool caps. It will be a miracle if
any of the boys who wore Peach and the Babke emerged from
childhood able to maintain an erection.

We often spent Isabel's lunch break in Pecan, a local coffee bar where we disturbed yuppies on laptops with our
incessant—and filthy—chatter.

"I can't find a goddamn fucking job and I'm too fat to be
a stripper," I said as I polished off a stale croissant.

Isabel paused as if contemplating an ad-
vanced theorem, then lit up. "We need another girl at Peach! We do, we do, we do!" It
would be a gas, she told me. It'd be like our
own secret clubhouse. "You can get tons of
free ribbons!" It was such an easy job. All you
had to do was fold, wrap, and minister to the
rich and famous. "That's all we did as kids,
be nice to art collectors so our parents could
pay our tuition," Isabel said. "You'll be amazing at it."

The next day, I stopped by with a copy of my résumé and
met Phoebe, the manager of the store, who looked like the
saddest fourth-grader you ever met but was, in reality, thirty-
two and none too pleased about it. She was beautiful like a
Gibson girl, a pale round face, heavy lids, and rosy lips. She
wiped her hands on her plaid pinafore.

"Why did you leave your last job?" she asked.

"I was hooking up with someone in the kitchen and the
dessert chef was a bitch," I explained.

"I can pay you one hundred dollars a day, cash," she said.

"Sounds good." I was secretly thrilled, both at the salary and the prospect of spending every day with my oldest and most amusing friends.

"We also buy you lunch every day," Phoebe said.

"The lunch is awesome!" Isabel chimed in, spreading some pint-sized leather gloves that retailed for $155 out in the display case next to a broken vintage camera (price upon request).

"I'm in," I said. For reasons I will never understand but did not question, Phoebe handed me twenty-five dollars for the interview itself.

And with that, Peach and the Babke became the most poorly staffed store in the history of the world.

The days at Peach and the Babke followed a certain rhythm. With only one window up front, it was hard to get a sense of time passing, and so life became a sedentary, if pleasant, mass of risotto and tiny overalls. But I will reconstruct it for you as best as I can:

**10:10** Roll in the door with a coffee in your hand. If you're feeling nice, you also bring one for Phoebe. "Sorry I'm late," you say before flinging your coat on the floor.

**10:40** Head into the back room to start casually folding some pima-cotton baby leggings ($55 to $65) and roll-neck fisherman sweaters ($175).

**10:50** Get distracted telling Joana a story about a homeless guy you saw wearing a salad spinner as a hat.

**11:10** First customer rings the bell. They are either freezing and looking to browse before their next appointment or obscenely rich and about to purchase five thousand dollars' worth of gifts for their nieces. You and Joana try to do the best wrapping job you can and to calculate the tax properly, but there is a good chance you charged them an extra five hundred dollars.

**11:15** Start talking about lunch. How badly you want or don't want it. How good it will be when it finally hits your lips or, alternately, how little mind you even pay to food these days.

**11:25** Call next door for the specials.

**12:00** Isabel arrives. She is on a schedule called Princess Hours. When you ask if you can also work Princess Hours, Phoebe says, "No, they're for princesses."

**12:30** Sit down for an elaborate three-course meal. Let Phoebe try your couscous, since it's the least you can do. Split a baguette with Isabel if you can have half her butternut squash soup. Eat a pot of fresh ricotta to finish it off.

**1:00** Joana leaves for therapy.

**1:30** The UPS guy comes and unloads boxes of rag dolls made of vintage curtains ($320). You ask him how his son is doing. He says he's in jail.

**2:00** Isabel leaves for therapy.

**2:30** Meg Ryan comes in wearing a large hat, buys nothing.

**3:00** Phoebe asks you to rub her head for a while. She lies on the rug in the back and moans with pleasure. A customer rings the doorbell. She says to ignore it, and when her massage is done she sends you around the corner for cappuccino and brownies.

**4:00** You leave for therapy, collecting your hundred dollars.

**6:00** This is the time work was actually supposed to end, but you are already home, half asleep, waiting for Jeff Ruiz to finish his landscaping job and meet you on the roof of his building to drink beer and feel each other up. Only once in nine months does Phoebe admonish you for your poor work ethic, and she feels so guilty about it that at lunch she goes across the street and buys you a scented candle.

Phoebe ran the store with her mother, Linda, though Linda spent most of her time in Pennsylvania or, if she was in the city, upstairs in the apartment she kept, smoking and eating popcorn from a big metal bowl. As thoughtful and conflicted as Phoebe was, her mother was so wild her hair stood on end. Phoebe handled the practicalities of the business, while Linda conceived designs so fantastical that rather than sketch them she would just wave ribbons and scraps in the air, outlining a sweater or a tutu. Phoebe and Linda's fights had a tendency to turn rabid and ranged from small-business issues to the very fiber of their characters.

"All my friends were getting abortions!" she screamed. Linda often spoke of her former life in San Francisco, pre-children, a utopia of knitwear designers and early Western practitioners of yoga who supported and inspired one another. The money was good, and the sex was even better.

As they fought, Isabel and I (or Joana and I, as it was rare we all worked at once) would look at each other nervously, shrug, then proceed to try on all the dresses we carried in a child's size 8, whose hemlines hit right below our crotches (aka just right). Another common distraction was to cover our heads in rabbit-fur barrettes ($16) or strap each other up with ribbons like some ersatz Helmut Newton photograph.

Sometimes I would find Phoebe crying by the air conditioner, head

on the desk where she kept her old PC, staring at a pile of unpaid bills. The fact was the store was in trouble. The recession was in full swing and, in times of economic hardship, high-end children's clothing is the first thing to go. We felt a deep and impenetrable sadness when we watched a hip-hop mogul's credit card get declined, a sure sign of doom for Peach and the Babke—and for the world.

Every day we hoped for a big sale, and every day we watched Phoebe's brow furrow as she went over the books, and every night we took our one-hundred-dollar bill home without reservation.

The job allowed us a lot of time for socializing. Together we were finding our own New York, which looked a lot like the New York of our parents. We went to art openings for the free wine and Christmas parties for the free food, then peeled off to smoke pot on Isabel's couch and watch reruns of *Seinfeld*. We stopped by parties where we didn't know the host, wore skirts as tube tops and tights as pants. We split bowls of Bolognese at chic restaurants rather than get full meals at boring ones. A night of carousing never passed without me stepping outside the experience to think, Yes, this must be what it is to be young.

Upon graduation I had felt a heavy sense of doom, a sense that nothing would ever be simple again. But look, look what we had found! We were making it work, with our cash and our bad wrapping jobs, with our fried overdyed hair and our fried overprocessed foods. Everything took on a hazy romance: having a pimple, eating a doughnut, being cold. Nothing was a tragedy, and everything was a joke. I had waited a long time to be a woman, a long time to venture away from my parents, and now I had sex, once with two guys in a week, and bragged about it like a divorcée who was getting back in the game. Up to my knees in mud from a night on the town, I rinsed off in the shower as Isabel watched and said, "Handle it, dirty girl!"

I didn't know the word for it, but I was happy. I was happy wrapping presents, catering to listless bankers' wives, and locking the store up with a rusty key a few minutes before closing time. I was happy being slightly condescending to people with platinum cards, reveling in our status as shopgirls who knew more than we were letting on. We would stay here in our cave, looking out on Tribeca through the picture window, and on weekends we would trip up the West Side Highway in red dresses, sloshing beer, ready to fuck and fight and fall asleep on top of one another.

But ambition is a funny thing: it creeps in when you least expect it and keeps you moving, even when you think you want to stay put. I missed making things, the meaning it gave this long march we call life. One night, as we readied ourselves for another event where we weren't exactly welcome, it occurred to me: This is something. Why didn't we tell this story, instead of just living it? The story of children of the art world trying (and failing) to match their parents' successes, unsure of their own passions, but sure they wanted glory. Why didn't we make a webseries (at that point, the Internet webseries was poised to replace film, television, radio, and literature) about characters even more pathetic than we were?

We never made it to the party that night. Instead we ordered pizza, curled up in easy chairs, and began pitching names and locations and plotlines into the night. We ransacked Isabel's closet for possible costume pieces (a beaded flapper dress, a Dudley Do-Right hat), and Joana conceived the hairstyle that would be her character's signature (a sleek beehive built around a shampoo bottle for height). And so, using the money that Peach and the Babke provided, we began to create something that would reflect the manic energy of this moment.

It was called *Delusional Downtown Divas,* a title we hated but couldn't top. Isabel portrayed AgNess, an aspiring businesswoman with a passion for power suits. Joana was the enigmatic Swann, a private performance artist. My character, Oona Winegrod, was an aspiring novelist who had never actually written a word. All of them were obsessed with a young painter named Jake Pheasant. We completed ten episodes, many of which featured cameos from our parents' friends, who still viewed us as children doing an adorable class project.

Looking at the videos now, they leave something to be desired. Blaringly digital, with shaky camerawork, we careen across the screen in messy costumes, cracking up at our own jokes, tickled with the ingenuity of our concept. Lines like "I just know we can join the feminist art collective if we put our minds to it and we will finally be IT girls!" are a little too real to feel like parody.

The first time I showed my father the footage, we were sitting at our dining room table. He took a long sip of tea, then asked, "Why did you have to do this?" And yes, it was broad, amateurish, a little vulgar. It didn't have narrative propulsion or cinematic graces. But watching it now, I can also feel the giddiness, the joy of creation we were all experiencing, the catharsis of admitting to our situation. It jumps off the screen.

It's silly and obvious and high on its own supply, but it's something. It's a step forward.

People who weren't my father kind of loved it, and we were invited to present the videos in a small gallery on Greene Street in Soho. In an attempt to remain staunchly rooted in the conceptual, we decided to decorate the gallery like a replica of Isabel's apartment. We hauled all our worldly possessions across Canal Street, including a treadmill, Isabel's couch, and some family heirlooms. We pulled all-nighters, decorating the space lovingly, and I insisted on wearing painter's overalls to complement my new identity as a serious artiste.

The night of our "opening" remains among the most surprising of my life: by the time I arrived (I was late, as my mother insisted I shower), the space was full, and the crowd was spilling into the street, wine in cups, feet in pirate boots and fluorescent heels. People we didn't even *know* were there, a testament to the idea that energy attracts energy, because our parents sure as hell weren't advertising. Someone asked to take our photograph. Isabel and Joana and I clutched at one another, unable to believe our luck. We went to a bar afterward, and a DJ gave me his business card in a way that could have been sexual. We had made it.

After that, life at Peach and the Babke lost some of its luster. Work induced a sleepy malaise, and I wondered if I had re-contracted mono. Joana got some illustration work and cut back on her hours. Isabel found increasing reasons not to appear. The walk across Hudson Street to open the store began to feel a little tragic.

Then one day, I botched the mailing list. I was meant to send out one thousand postcards heralding our summer sample sale. But, caught up in a reverie, I didn't notice I had printed five hundred address stickers for one single family and applied nearly all of them. My error was so shocking to Linda that her nostrils flared and spit flew as she screamed at me.

"I'm sorry," I told her. "But I have a bus to catch."

I boarded a Greyhound to Ithaca to see a college friend, the kind of purposeless trip you will never take again after age twenty-five. We spent the weekend walking in fields, taking pictures of old-fashioned neon signs with a disposable camera, and watching carp spawn in a river. We ate nothing but hummus and drank nothing but beer. We went to his neighbor's funeral and sat in the back row and got the giggles, sprinted out. We walked around his mother's garden, crushing living things with our boots.

"How's your job?" he asked.

"My boss is such a bitch," I told him.

I projected onto his life a sweetness, a lack of complication, the kind of vibe terrible people would call "quaint." I loved his basement apartment in a ramshackle house, the fact that there was only one Chinese restaurant in town, and that he'd never have to see a more successful person than himself at a party. I was jealous. I wanted to be in it. I wanted to fuck it up.

So, on the night before I left, I drank half a whiskey ginger and hurled my naked body onto his, kissing him in an unfocused but enthusiastic way. He responded with a sad smile, and we fucked in the blue light of a documentary about police brutality. We didn't speak for a year, but I thought of his house all the time.

In September of 2009 the Delusional Downtown Divas were offered our first real gig: hosting the Guggenheim's First Annual Art Awards. Our parents were shocked that this lark had brought anyone even remotely serious knocking on our door, but I've always believed that it turns people on to get made fun of, and the art world was no exception. We were offered license to run wild and a five-thousand-dollar fee to split among us. We all quit our jobs at Peach and the Babke that day with the joyful abandon of lottery winners.

I rented a hundred-square-foot office in a nearby building, which became our official headquarters, and set to work. The building was populated with young handsome filmmakers in porkpie hats and professionals who couldn't quite explain what they did. People built half-pipes in their offices and encouraged interoffice sleepovers. Everyone bought their lunch from a deli called New Fancy Food. The landlord, a Chinese woman named Summer Weinberg, asked sweetly whether I was a prostitute. Our minifridge had nothing but *tres leches* cake in it.

We spent months preparing, creating new episodes and writing awards-show-style banter about figures like performance artist Joan Jonas ("Is she the Jonas Brothers' mother?"). We shot an episode in the museum itself and were almost removed after I encouraged Isabel to hang her leg over the mezzanine and scream, "I'm gonna pull a Carl Andre up here!"

The awards themselves were a blur. We awoke early and traveled uptown to have our hair styled professionally for the first time. We hit our marks and heard our voices echo up to the rotunda. We saw James Franco, something that now seems hard to avoid. During intermission Isabel and I got into a tearful fight when I told a makeup artist that Isabel "ought to own a store."

"You don't believe in me," she said. "You don't think I

know how to do anything real, which is the only reason you would ever tell someone to open a store."

"Yes, I do. Look at all this!" I cried.

"Yeah, but we're not going to, like, do this for our *lives*," Joana said.

In the months that followed, we dispersed: me to Los Angeles, Joana to graduate school, Isabel to upstate New York, where she met a man named Jason with a sweet smile and no connection to the art world whatsoever. We took the videos we had made together off the Internet, embarrassed by the things we had once thought so profound.

"What's the worst job you've ever had?" is a popular question in interviews and at dinner parties.

"Once my boss yelled at me for giving Gwyneth Paltrow the wrong size in baby leggings," I say, wincing at the memory. What I don't say is that it felt like home, that it started our journey, that we ate the best lunches I've ever had. What I don't say is that I miss it.

# *17 Things I Learned from My Father*

**1.** Death is coming for us all.

**2.** There are no bad thoughts, only bad actions.

**3.** "Men, watch out: the ladies are coming for your toys."

**4.** Confidence lets you pull anything off, even Tevas with socks.

**5.** All children are amazing artists. It's the grown-ups you have to worry about.

**6.** Unhappy at a party? Say you're going to check on your car, then exit swiftly. Make eye contact with no one.

**7.** Drunk emotions aren't real emotions.

**8.** A sweet potato prepared in the microwave, then slathered with flaxseed oil, makes for an exceptional snack.

**9.** It's never too late to learn.

**10.** "The Volvo is bad enough. I'm not putting a coat on the fucking dog."

**11.** A rising tide lifts all boats.

**12.** That being said, it's horrible when people you hate get things you want.

**13.** Hitting a creative wall? Take a break from work to watch a procedural. They always solve the case, and so will you.

**14.** You don't need to be flamboyant in your life to be flamboyant in your work.

**15.** Wear a suit to the DMV to speed things along a bit.

**16.** Do not make jokes about concealing drugs, weapons, or currency in front of police officers or TSA workers. There is nothing funny about being detained.

**17.** It's all about tailoring.

# *Emails I Would Send If I Were One Ounce Crazier/Angrier/Braver*

Dear Blanken Blankstein,
Remember when I ran into you last summer at the coffee place near your house? I was with a bunch of guys from my work and you were with some guys from yours. Some of them wore "wifebeaters" and looked like wife beaters. I was rendered speechless by your tangled Rip Van Winkle beard, which I didn't get close enough to smell but can imagine presents massive hygiene challenges. It clearly took major effort to grow, and that is the biggest signal I've received to date that your emotional equilibrium is off. I shook like a dry drunk because I was so scared you'd yell at me for the thing I wrote about you. I said sorry a lot that day. Your expression was so stormy, I just wanted to calm you down. Plus, I was trying to be adult around my cowork-

ers, a concept you would know nothing about, you coke-nosed dick-swinger.

But I'm actually *not sorry at all.* You weren't kind to me, so I have nothing to be sorry about. I'm sick of saying stuff I don't mean.

As you were,

Lena

p.s. All *my* work friends thought you looked like a puppet of a hipster. Your pants are so high waisted I could cry. I don't care what your work friends thought of me. I hadn't showered in four days and I still have a boyfriend last I checked.

———

Dear Dr. Blank,

My eardrum was *punctured,* you WHITECOAT. And you treated me like a psycho with a little scrape, like an exhausting roadblock between you and your lunch. I cried when you poured the solution down my earhole and you just held me in place. I had to beg for painkillers like a junkie. Who gave you a license? This has since become my most traumatic memory, usurping the premature death of a friend and the time I saw a woman with a gaping pink hole where her nose ought to be. I resent that.

Lena

———

Dear Mrs. Blank,

You are literally schizophrenic, so it's futile to answer your email, BUT I gotta say: you are bananas. I understand that you come from a generation of women who had to work hard to be heard, but for you to impugn my feminism and

act as though I'm a scourge upon women everywhere, just because I refuse to spread *your* particular agenda? That's dark, and it's not what you fought for. If you continue this way, you're worse than they are (they = men). We are all just trying to get by. There is room for all of us. Also, "cudgeled" isn't a word people use. I'm going to live at least fifty years past you.
Sincerely,
Lena

———

Dear Blanka,
Remember when you said you "forgave" me for my movie? Well, I don't forgive you for saying that. I am sorry that I questioned whether you were a real lesbian. That was lame of me and you clearly are a lesbian. I love lesbians. But you know what else is lame? Your neon overalls. D. J. Tanner called and she wants her wardrobe back so it can be included in a museum retrospective about the prime years of *Full House*.
Ugh, get it together!
LD

———

Dear Blanky Blankham,
We had been friends since fourth grade. You used to bring flowers to my screen door, take me out on the lake in your dinghy, show me how to catch frogs. We had a childhood together. So when I gave you a blow job (MY FIRST) on the day my cat died, you should have called. Your total disappearance made so many sweet memories feel so grimy.

I found out about your fiancée on Facebook. How many inches taller than you is she? Like, ten? The fact that the government lets you fly planes seems insane.

Your little friend,

Lena

p.s. I never picked up the cat's ashes because I associated it with giving blow jobs and being abandoned. When I finally got up the courage to collect them two years later, they had been thrown into a mass grave. I blame you.

# I Didn't Fuck Them, but They Yelled at Me

THIS IS THE NAME of the memoir I'm going to write when I'm eighty. You know, once everyone I've met in Hollywood is dead.

It will be a look back at an era when women in Hollywood were treated like the paper thingies that protect glasses in hotel bathrooms—necessary but infinitely disposable.

It will be excerpted in *Vanity Fair* along with photos of me laughing at a long-ago premiere, wearing a pom-pom strapped to my head, sipping a cran and seltzer, subtly pregnant with my first set of twins.

It will be endorsed by the female president, and I'll enjoy a real surge in popularity with college girls writing term papers on the history of the gender gap.

I can't wait to be eighty.

So I can have an "oeuvre"—or at least a "filmography."

So I can impress my grandkids with my brooch collection.

So I can send things back in restaurants without shame and use a wheelchair at the airport.

So I can shock people by saying "rim job" in casual conversation.

So I can dye my bowl cut orange.

And so I can name names. Delicious, vengeful names. And I won't give a shit about doing battle with someone's estate because I'll be eighty and, quite possibly, the owner of seventeen swans.

I'll tell everyone about what the men I met in Hollywood said to me that first whirlwind year:

"I just want to protect you."

"I know we just met, but I consider you a close friend."

"You're a funny girl."

"You're a clever kid."

"I'll bet you never say no."

"You should be a little more grateful."

"You're prettier than you let yourself be."

"I hope your boyfriend makes you feel good. You have a boyfriend, don't you?"

"You know, a lot of men can't handle a powerful woman. . . ."

"You've grown very cute since I last ran into you."

I'll recount all the interactions where I went from having an engaging conversation on craft with a man to hearing about his sexual dissatisfaction with his wife, who used to be passionate and is currently on fertility drugs. Suddenly, we're talking about the way his college girlfriend left her boots on when she fucked and how marriage is "a lot of hard work."

What that translates to is: *My wife doesn't turn me on and you aren't a model but you sure are young and probably some bold new sexual moves have emerged since the last time I was single in 1992 so let's try it and then you can go back to being married to your work and I'll go back to being married to an "eco-friendly interior decorator" and I'll never watch any of your films again.*

I'll talk about how I never fucked any of them. I fucked guys who lived in vans, guys who shared illegal lofts with their ex-girlfriends who were away at Coachella, guys who were into indigenous plant life, and guys who watched PBS.

But I never fucked *them.*

I'll talk about the way these relationships fell apart as soon as they realized I wasn't going to be anyone's protégée, pet, private fan club, or eager plus-one.

The subtle accusation: "You're not so easy to track down."

The sensitive inquiry: "What's goin' on here, honey?"

The rageful indictment: "You're a bullshit liar. Doesn't anyone your age have any fucking manners?"

My friend Jenni calls them Sunshine Stealers. Men who have been at it a little too long, who are tired of the ride but can't get off. They're looking for some new form of energy, of approval. It's linked with sex, but it's not the same. What they want to take from you is way worse than your thong in the back of their Lexus. It's ideas, curiosity, an excitement about getting up in the morning and making things.

"Oh," she'll tell me when I mention the only guy I talked to at a boring dinner party. "Another Sunshine Stealer."

"That one," she says about a seemingly charming visionary. "He's the OG Sunshine Stealer."

When I'm eighty, I'll describe the time I sat with a director in his hotel suite while he told me girls love it when you "direct" their blow jobs.

"Oh, wow," I answered. I mean, how else do you answer?

"I don't know," he said. "They just dig it."

I'll describe the pseudo-date I went on with a man whose work I admired. I wore a white dress with only one stain, and we barreled downtown in a cab, and I leaned back against the torn pleather seat and thought, I've really done it, I'm a grown-ass woman now. And at 4:00 A.M. when I tried to kiss him he stayed stone faced. I hit his side mouth, and I turned on my heels and took off down the block at a speed I've never achieved before or since. I felt so ashamed. My first and only misstep of this kind, and he'd be able to tell them all: *She's weak, she's just like the rest of them. She wants it.*

I'll describe another, even-older filmmaker and how, following him down the street after a drink, I realized that he limped a little, unexplained. And I'll describe the email he wrote me after I said I couldn't work on his film because I was making my own show. "How could you dismiss this opportunity to be a small part of a film that will be taught in colleges for years to come in exchange for the utter ephemera of a 'TV Pilot.'" In quotes! He put it IN QUOTES!

And I read the email again and again, shocked, jaw set with rage so that I couldn't make a sound. And I imagined my own pain, my anger, magnified by fifty in the man who would send that email, the person who believes that life is a zero-sum game and girls are there to be your props, that anyone else's artistry is a mere distraction from the Lord's grand plan to promote your agenda. How painful that must be, how suffocating. And I decided then that I will never be jealous. I will never be vengeful. I won't be threatened by the old, or by the new. I'll open wide like a daisy every morning. I will make my work.

I've imagined the Sunshine Stealers, around a long conference table like the members of the Cabinet, in dialogue about me. *She's sly and manipulative,* one says. *She'll do anything to get what she wants,* says another. *You have to be a hell of a lot prettier than* that *to fuck your way to the top.* An especially old one chimes in: *I had some great times with her, man, nice girl, wonder what'll become of her.*

But the scariest thought of all is the one that pushed me to keep making contact well past the point that I became uncomfortable, to try and prove myself again and again. The reason I didn't stop answering their calls, that I rushed to drinks dates that were past my bedtime and had conversations that didn't interest me and forced myself to sit at the table long after I'd grown uncomfortable. The thought I worked so vigilantly to ensure they would never entertain: *She's silly. She's no threat.*

My friend, a woman whom I admire for her independent spirit, told me she had a similar experience. "I made my first movie and all these men crawled out of the woodwork, looking for . . . something." She was once a punk. The real kind, not the kind who buys her clothes at the mall. "But they didn't get it: I'm not here to make friends with you. I'm here to destroy you."

I told her I was out of the danger zone now, but for a moment there my phone ringing at 2:00 A.M. became an instrument of terror. Who had my number that didn't know how to use it appropriately? A message, delivered in low tones: "If you have a moment, I'd love to talk. You're a good listener."

You know why I listened? Because I wanted it so bad. Because I wanted to learn, to grow and to *stay*.

*Oh, look,* they said to themselves, *it's a cute little director-shaped thing.*

Just wait until I'm eighty.

# SECTION V
# *Big Picture*

# Therapy & Me

I AM EIGHT and I am afraid of everything.

The list of things that keep me up at night includes, but is not limited to: appendicitis, typhoid, leprosy, unclean meat, foods I haven't seen emerge from their packaging, foods my mother hasn't tasted first so that if we die we die together, homeless people, headaches, rape, kidnapping, milk, the subway, sleep.

An assistant teacher comes to school with bloodshot eyes, and I am convinced he's infected with Ebola. I wait for blood to trickle from his ear or for him to just fall down dead. I stop touching my shoelaces (too filthy) or hugging adults outside of my family. In school, we are learning about Hiroshima, so I read *Sadako and the Thousand Paper Cranes* and I know instantly that I have leukemia. A symptom of leukemia is dizziness and I have that, when I sit up too fast or spin around in circles. So I quietly prepare to die in the next year or so, depending on how fast the disease progresses.

My parents are getting worried. It's hard enough to have a child, much less a child who demands to inspect our groceries and medicines for evidence that their protective seals have been tampered with. I have only the vaguest memory of a life before fear. Every morning when I wake up there is one blissful second before I look around the room and remember my daily terrors. I wonder if this is what it will always be like, forever, and I try to remember moments I felt safe: In bed next to my mother one Sunday morning. Playing with Isabel's puppy. Getting picked up from a sleepover just before bedtime.

One night my father becomes so frustrated by my behavior that he takes a walk and doesn't come back for three hours. While he's gone, I start to plan our life without him.

My fourth-grade teacher, Kathy, is my best friend at school. She's a plump, pretty woman with hair like yellow pipe cleaners. Her clothes resemble the sheets at my grandma's house, threadbare florals with mismatched buttons. She says I can ask her as many questions as I want: about tidal waves, about my sinuses, about nuclear war. She offers vague, reassuring answers. In hindsight they were tinged with religion, implied a faith in a distinctly Christian God. She can tell when I'm getting squirrelly, and she shoots me a look across the room that says, *It's okay, Lena, just give it a second.*

When I'm not with Kathy I'm with Terri Mangiano, our school nurse, who has a buzz cut and a penchant for wearing holiday sweaters all year round. She has a no-nonsense approach to health that comforts me. She presents me with statistics (only 2 percent of children develop Reye's syndrome in response to aspirin) and tells me that polio has been eradicated. She takes me seriously when I explain that I've been exposed to scarlet fever by a kid on the subway with a red face. Sometimes she lets me lie on the top bunk in the back room, dark and cool. I rest my cheek against the plastic mattress cover and listen to her administer pills and pregnancy tests to high school girls. If I'm lucky, she doesn't send me back to class.

No one likes the way things are going so, at some point, therapy is suggested. I am used to appointments: allergist, chiropractor, tutor. All I want is to feel better, and that overrides the fear of something new, something reserved for people who are crazy. Plus, both my parents have therapists, and I feel more like my parents than anybody else. My father's therapist is named Ruth. I've never met her, but I asked him to describe her to me once. He said she was older, but not as old as Grandma, with longish gray hair. In my head, her office has no windows, it's just a box with two chairs. I wonder what Ruth thinks of me. He has to have said *something*.

"Can't I just see Ruth?" I ask. He explains that it doesn't work that way, that I need my own place to have my own private thoughts. So I take the train uptown with him to meet someone of my own. For some reason, when we go to appointments to help my mind, it's always my father who comes. My mother comes to the ones for my body.

The first doctor, a violet-haired grandma-aged woman with a German surname, asks me a few simple questions and then invites me to play with the toys scattered across her floor. She sits in a chair above me, pad in hand. I have the sense she will gather all kinds of information from this, so I put on a show that I'm sure will demonstrate my loneliness and introspection: Bootleg Barbie crashes her convertible with off-brand Ken riding shotgun. Tiny Lego men are killed in a war against their own kind. After a long period of observation, she asks me to share my three greatest wishes. "A river, where I can be alone," I tell her, impressed with my own poeticism. From this answer, she will know that I am not like other nine-year-olds.

"And what else?" she asks.

"That's all."

I leave feeling worse than when I went in, and my father says that's okay, we can see as many doctors as we need to until I'm better. Next we visit a different woman, even older than the first, but she's named Annie, which is not an old person's name. We walk up four or five flights to her office, which is also her living room. My father sits with me this time and helps me explain the things that worry me. Annie is sympathetic, with a funny high laugh, and when we walk out into the night on Bank Street, I tell my father she is the one.

But we are just here to get a referral, my father tells me. Annie is retiring.

And so my third session is with Robyn. Robyn's office is down the block from our apartment and, sensing some trepidation, my mother pulls me aside and says to think of it like a play date. If I like playing with her, I can go back. If not, we'll find someone else for me to play with. I nod, but I'm well aware that most play dates don't revolve around someone trying to figure out whether you're crazy or not.

In our first session, Robyn sits on the floor with me, her legs tucked under her like she's just a friend who has come by to hang out. She looks like the mom on a television show, with big curly hair and a silky blouse. She asks me how old I am, and I respond by asking her how old she is—after all, we're sitting on the floor together. "Thirty-four," she says. My mother was thirty-six when I was *born*. Robyn is different from my mother in lots of ways, starting with her clothes: a skirt-suit, sheer tights, and clean black high heels. Different from my mother, who looks like her normal self when she dresses as a witch for Halloween.

Robyn lets me ask her whatever I want. She has two daughters. She lives uptown. She's Jewish. Her middle name is Laura, and her favorite food is cereal. By the time I leave, I think that she could fix me.

The germophobia morphs into hypochondria morphs into sexual anxiety morphs into the pain and angst that accompany entry into middle school. Over time, Robyn and I develop a shorthand for things I'm too embarrassed to say: "Masturbation" becomes "M," "sexuality" becomes "ooality," and my crushes become "him." I don't like the term "gray area," as in "the gray area between being scared and aroused," so Robyn coins "the pink area." We eventually move into her adult office but stay sitting on the floor. We'll often share a box of Special K or a croissant.

She teaches me how to needlepoint, abstract geometric designs in autumnal threads. When I turn thirteen she throws me a private atheistic Bat Mitzvah—just us two—where we eat half a pound of prosciutto. She tells me that soon she'll be getting a real Bat Mitzvah, even though she's almost forty now.

One evening I see her on the subway, and our interaction, warm but disorienting, inspires a poem, the last lines of which are: "I guess you are not my mother. You will never be my mother." I make her a painting, a girl with big Keane eyes crying violet tears, and she tells me that she's hung it in her bathroom, along with a free-form nude I did using gouache.

I bring my disposable camera and take pictures of us hanging out and drawing, just like pals do.

The work we're doing together helps, but even three mornings a week isn't enough to stop the terrible thoughts, the fear of sleep and of life in general. Sometimes, to manage the images that come unbidden, I force myself to picture my parents copulating in intricate patterns, summoning the image in sets of eight, for so long that looking at them makes me nauseous.

"Mom," I say. "Turn away from me so I won't think of sex."

Sitting with my mother in the beauty salon one afternoon, I come across an article about obsessive-compulsive disorder. A woman describes her life, so burdened with obsessions that she has to lick art in museums and crawl on the sidewalk. Her symptoms aren't much worse than mine: the magazine's description of her most horrible day parallels my average one. I tear the article out and bring it to Robyn, whose face crumples sympathetically, as though the moment she'd been dreading had finally arrived. It makes me want to throw my needlepoint supplies in her face. Do I have to do everything myself?

One day, when I'm fourteen, Robyn warns me that she might get an important call during our session. She's sorry, but she has to take it, wouldn't do it if it wasn't a real emergency. She's gone for about ten minutes, and when she returns she looks rattled. Takes a deep breath. "So—"

"Where's your wedding ring?" I ask her.

"I'll see you Wednesday, Leen," Robyn says, and I pull on my orange parka and head for the elevator. In the waiting room are two teenagers—a blond boy, the kind of underdeveloped but cute thirteen-year-old male that drives seventh-grade gals crazy despite being four-foot-seven, and a pale girl with green streaks in her hair. I stare at her for a moment too long, because I recognize her: she's the one in the photo in Robyn's Filofax, which sometimes lies open on her desk. That's Robyn's daughter, Audrey.

I leave the office a beat before they do, but they catch up with me at the elevator, and I'm holding my breath as we ride down together, trying to somehow take her in without looking directly at her. I wish she were a picture in a magazine, so I could stare, rotate the page slightly, stare again.

Does she know who I am? Maybe she's jealous. I would be. When we reach the ground floor, she looks right into my face. "He thinks you're hot," she says, motioning to her friend, then bolts.

I step out onto Broadway, beaming.

·　☕　·

What happens over the next few months is like the plot of a children's movie, the kind where a dog finds its owner in spite of insurmountable odds and prohibitive geography. Through shrewd detective work, Audrey discovers that her camp friend Sarah is *my* school friend Sarah, and begins passing me notes. They are fat envelopes, decorated with puff paint and star stickers. Inside the first one is a letter, in the kind of fun teen scrawl they use in *Saved by the Bell:* "HEY

From: Audrey
To: Lena ♡

YOU SEEM AWESOME! I bet we'd get along. My mom says we would if we could meet. I love shopping, the *Felicity* soundtrack, oh, and shopping. Here's a pic of me at the Wailing Wall after my Bat Mitzvah! INSTANT MESSAGE MEEEE."

I write back an equally effusive note, laboring over which picture to share, before finally settling on a shot of me lounging on my sister's bunk bed in a vintage crop top that reads SUPER DEBBIE. "I also luuuv the *Felicity* soundtrack, animals, acting, and DUH SHOPPING! My screen name is LA-FEMMELENA."

I know our correspondence is wrong, and so I tell Robyn, who confirms my belief that this is inappropriate. "It's too bad," she says, "because I think you two are very similar. You would probably be good friends."

·  🐌  ·

When I'm fifteen I stop working with Robyn. I'm ready to stop talking about my problems all the time, I tell her, and she doesn't fight me. I feel good. My OCD isn't completely gone, but maybe it never will be. Maybe it's part of who I am, part of what I have to manage, the challenge of my life. And for now that seems okay.

Our last session is full of laughter, fancy snacks, talk of the future. I admit how much it hurt me when she reacted with disgust to my belly-button ring, and she says she's sorry she displayed her personal bias. I thank her for having let me bring my cat into a session and for removing said belly-button ring once it became infected, using a pair of pliers, and, most of all, for having guided me toward wellness. For the first time in many years, I have secrets. Thoughts that aren't suitable for anyone but me.

I miss her the way I missed our loft after we moved in seventh grade: sharply, and then not at all. There is too much unpacking to do.

🍎

Within six months, I'm ignoring my homework and skipping class so I can hang out with my pet rabbit Chester Hadley. My parents think I'm depressed, and I think they're idiots. Because of my medication, I'm sleepy all the time, and I become notorious at school for napping in my hood, snapping to attention the moment a teacher says my name: "I wasn't sleeping."

My fascination with Robyn's daughter has never died, and our lives overlap just enough that I have a sense of where and how she is: I'm told she pierced her own nose at summer camp and is dating a graffiti artist named SEX. Once, our mutual friend puts us on the phone together, and I can barely speak.

"Hey!" she growls.

"It's you," I say.

⌐

My struggle is deepening, and my father tells me that I am going to see Margaret, a "learning and organization" specialist who I met with a few times years earlier when my parents discovered I had been stuffing all my unfinished homework under my bed for half the school year. I remember her fondly enough, mostly because she offered Chessmen cookies and orange juice before we set to work on my math homework. When I arrive this time, she doesn't offer any cookies, but she looks just as I'd left her: wavy red bob, creatively draped black dress, and witch boots. More like my mother than Robyn, but with an Australian accent.

Her office is a museum of pleasing curiosities: framed seashells, dried pussy willows extending from asymmetrical vases, a coffee table decorated with feathers and stray tiles used as coasters. For a few weeks, we sit at her desk and focus on organizing my backpack, which looks like a crack-addicted hoarder with five toddlers took up residence in its front zipper pocket. She shows me how to keep a datebook and label the sections of a binder and check assignments off when I've finished them. Margaret is a psychiatrist as well, and I often see sad children or mismatched couples waiting for her after our session, but this isn't the place to talk about my feelings. We are all about efficiency, neat edges, prioritizing.

But one day I come in, melted down by a recurrence of obsessive thoughts and by the milky, sickening feeling my medication is giving me. I don't have the will to clean out my binder. I had gotten such satisfaction out of the systems she introduced, the sharp pencils and crisp manila folders. But, in a grand metaphor for my worsening state, I have doodled nonsense on all the once-pristine pages. I lay my head on the desk.

"Do you want to sit on the couch?" Margaret asks.

·  &#8505;  ·

Margaret won't tell me anything about her life. From the start, she makes it clear that we're here to talk about me. When I ask a question about herself, she tends to ignore it. She isn't mean about it. Rather, she looks at me with a blank smile that implies I've spoken to her in a language she doesn't understand.

"Just curious, do you have children?" I ask.

"What do you think knowing the answer to that would do for you?" she asks me, just like shrinks do in movies.

As a result of her reticence, I develop my own theories about Margaret. One is that she's a measured and reasonable eater, unable to understand my personal battle with gluttony. I have seen a goat's milk yogurt in her garbage before, the lid placed neatly back on the empty carton. Another of my theories is that she loves a warm bath. I am sure she loves wildflowers, trains, and heart-to-hearts with wise old women. One day she tells me that as a schoolgirl she was forced to wear a boater hat on field trips. I cling to this image, imagining a tiny Margaret marching to and fro in a long line of girls in hats.

Then there is the autumn day I come in to find her with a bright, shiny black eye. Before I can even register my shock, she points to it and laughs. "A bit of a gardening accident." But I believe her. Margaret would never let anyone hit her. She would never let anyone wear shoes indoors. She would always protect herself, her floors, her flowers.

My father says his friend Burt knew Margaret in the nineties, that she had been "around for a minute," having a dalliance with a video artist. I imagine their dates: he slides into the booth across from her and asks her how her day was. She just smiles and nods, smiles and nods.

That Audrey and I wind up at college together is one of the strangest things that has happened, maybe ever, but definitely to me. On the surface, it makes perfect sense: two New York City girls with similar SAT scores and similar authority problems being directed toward the same attainable liberal education by uncreative administrators. But spiritually, I can't believe it. After all these years of separateness, we are together.

We bond immediately, more over what we hate than what we love. We both hate lox. We both hate boys in cargo pants. We're both sick of kids from Long Island saying they're from New York. We spend the first few weeks of the school year riding our new red bicycles around town in impractical shoes and too much lipstick, unwilling to let go of the idea that city girls do it differently. We can barely hold in our peals of laughter when a boy named Zenith arrives at a party in a shirt that says B IS FOR BALLER. We set our sights on senior boys who run ironic literary magazines and try to avoid using the bathroom next to anybody but each other.

Audrey is an intellectual, likes to talk about Fellini and read thick books about tainted presidencies by old bearded men. But she also uses slang more confidently than I ever could and holds her denim miniskirt together with patches from hard-core shows. She cuts her own hair, applies her own liquid eyeliner, and appears to be able to eat as many cookies as she wants without breaking one hundred pounds. We make up funny names for each other: *sqeedly-doo, looty, boober.*

We have our first fight three weeks in, when I decide she's holding me back socially with her misanthropy. "I came here to grow," I tell her. "And you don't want that."

She runs into the woods of the arboretum sobbing, falls, and scrapes her knee. When I try to help, she cries, "Why would you want to!?"

I call my mother, who is on Ambien and cheerfully tells me to just "buy a ticket home!" I feel certain and terrified that Audrey is in her room talking to her mother, and that Robyn is mad at me.

We make up a few days later when, at a brunch potluck, I realize that I do, in fact, hate everybody. Even my new friend Allison, who runs the radio station, and even Becky, who makes vegan muffins and has a quilt composed of Clash t-shirts. The conversation at college is making me insane: politically correct posturing by people without real politics. Audrey was right: we are all that is good for each other.

Sometimes Audrey and I are eating cereal, or drying off after the shower, and I see a flash of her mother. Robyn is here: young and naked, my friend.

Margaret is on vacation, and it's an emergency. My mother and I are in the worst fight we've ever had, one that tests the concept of unconditional love, not to mention basic human decency. And the thing is, no one is right exactly. We both followed our hearts and had no choice but to hurt each other deeply.

I try Margaret, but, as this is not technically a life-threatening emergency, I don't leave a message. Next I call my aunt, who I hope will at least tell me I am not a sack of rancid garbage shaped like a human.

"Your mom isn't easy, and neither are you," she says. "I don't know how you'll fix it, I just know that you have to." She suggests I call her friend, "relationship expert" Dr. Linda Jordan. "Linda will have thoughts," she promises. "And she is great with giving fast and efficient advice."

Advice? My therapist has never given me advice. She's all about making me give *myself* advice.

So, about to commit my second major betrayal since the one my mother can tell you all about, I call someone else's therapist.

Relationship Expert Dr. Linda Jordan is on a trip to Washington, D.C., with friends from college, so she calls me back from a bench outside the Smithsonian. It turns out we've met—years ago, at a Bat Mitzvah—and I vaguely remember her cap of honey hair and a handful of chunky diamond rings. "So, what's going on?" she asks, with the warm but solution-oriented tone of a high-powered divorce attorney.

I let it all pour out. What I did. What my mother did back. What we'd both done to each other since we did those first things that we did. "Uh-huh, uh-huh," Linda says, letting me know she's with me.

Finally, I breathe. "So. Am I terrible?"

For the next twenty minutes, Linda talks. First, she explains some basic "facts" about the mother-daughter relationship. ("You are her possession, but you are also a person.") Next, she tells me that we've both behaved in perfectly understandable, if unpleasant, ways. ("I get it" is a favorite phrase.) "So," she concludes. "This is actually a chance to reach the next phase of your bond if you will let it be. I know that you can come out of this stronger than before if you can tell her, 'You're my mother, and I need you, but in a different way than before. Please let us change, together.' "

I hang up and feel the panic subside for the first time in days: Relationship Expert Dr. Linda Jordan has helped me. And fast. It wasn't like Margaret, where I talk around something and she nods and we discuss a Henry James novel I've only read part of and then we meander back to the topic of my grandmother and how I'd kill to be asleep and then I compliment her shoes, which are, as always, fabulous. I asked a question and Dr. Linda Jordan gave me an answer. And now I have the tools to fix it.

I hang up the phone and call my mother: "I love you," I

say. "You're my mother, and I need you, but in a different way than before. Please let us change, together."

"That's fucking bullshit," she says. I can tell she's in a store.

·  ~~  ·

Audrey has had fifteen sinus infections this winter alone so, doctor's orders, she is having her nose broken, septum straightened, tonsils and adenoids removed. Five of us troop uptown to Robyn's apartment, where Audrey is recuperating. Before we ring the doorbell we put on Groucho glasses with attached noses and hold up our jug of soup.

Robyn answers in yoga pants. "The patient is this way," she says.

Audrey lies on Robyn's four-poster bed, nose bandaged, looking even tinier than usual. Robyn climbs onto the bed beside her. "How you feeling, sweetie?"

The other girls head to the kitchen to unpack the magazines and cookies we bought from a kiosk in the subway. And, as if we've done it fifty times before, as if we are a family, I crawl into bed with Audrey and Robyn. We all need to be taken care of sometimes.

·  🍬  ·

Margaret and I have talked on the phone from just about everywhere. I've called her from beaches, speeding vehicles in western states, crouched behind a Dumpster, in the parking lot of my college dormitory, and from my bedroom ten blocks from her office, when I didn't have the energy to make my way to her couch. From Europe, Japan, and Israel. I've whispered to her about guys who were sleeping next to me.

Never has the sound of her voice, that calm but expectant hello, not put me at ease. She answers on the second ring, and all my muscles and veins relax.

On a recent vacation, I call her from the Arizona desert, wearing only my underwear, baking my flesh by a plunge pool. I spend the majority of our session telling her about the furniture shopping my boyfriend and I have done that morning. Our first time making real aesthetic choices as a couple, we successfully selected a coffee table, two bronze deer, and a pair of torn leatherette barstools. Unable to resist, I threw a Cubist ceramic cat into the mix.

"I really feel like we have similar taste!" I gush, ignoring how unsure she sounds about the addition of kitschy metal animals to a living room.

"That's wonderful," she says. "My husband and I have always had similar taste and it really makes creating a home such a pleasure." With her accent, "pleasure" sounds like *pleeeshuh. Such a pleeshuh.*

Stunned, I wait a beat.

"It does!" I say. She told me. She told me. *She told me.*

Later in the conversation, she references a trip to Paris: "For my husband's job we go quite regularly." This is like Christmas. Gift after gift. Not only do I now know she has a husband, I know he is quite possibly French or at the very least EMPLOYED BY FRENCH PEOPLE. This is information I can work with. Next she is going to tell me about her Black Panther college boyfriend and her miscarriage and her best friend, Joan.

"HUGE NEWS!" I tell everyone who will listen. "My therapist has a husband. And he *might be French.*"

Why does Margaret deem me ready now? What test have I passed, what maturity have I displayed? Do therapists have a metric by which they judge our ability to work with information rationally? I wonder if she regretted it when she hung up, frowned, and gathered up her pretty hands, the hands with a gold ring on every finger so as to keep the mystery alive.

Maybe I have properly conveyed the truth and security of my romantic relationship and she is ready to admit me into a club of stable, balanced women with whom she shares. Maybe she just can't resist gabbing when it comes to midcentury furnishings. Or maybe it was an accident. Maybe she forgot our roles for a moment, and we became just two women, two friends on a long-distance call. Catching up about our houses, our husbands, our lives.

# Is This Even Real?

*Thoughts on Death & Dying*

I THINK A FAIR AMOUNT about the fact that we're all going to die. It occurs to me at incredibly inopportune moments—I'll be standing in a bar, having managed to get an attractive guy to laugh, and I'll be laughing, too, and maybe dancing a little bit, and then everything goes slo-mo for a second and I'll think: Are these people aware that we're all going to the same place in the end? I can slip back into conversation and tell myself that the flash of mortality awareness has enriched my experience, reminded me to just go for it in the giggling and hair-flipping and speaking-my-mind departments because . . . why the hell not? But occasionally the feeling stays with me, and it reminds me of being a child—feeling full of fear but lacking the language to calm yourself down. I guess, when it comes to death, none of us really has the words.

I wish I could be one of those young people who seems totally unaware of the fact that her gleaming nubile body is, in fact, fallible. (Maybe you have to have a gleaming nubile body to feel that way.) Beautiful self-delusion: Isn't that what being young is all about? You think you're immortal until one day when you're around sixty, it hits you: you see an Ingmar Bergman–y specter of death and you do some soul searching and possibly adopt a kid in need. You resolve to live the rest of your life in a way you can be proud of.

But I am not one of those young people. I've been obsessed with death since I was born.

As a little kid, an unnamed fear would often overtake me. It wasn't a fear of anything tangible—tigers, burglars, homelessness—and it couldn't be solved by usual means like hugging my mother or turning on Nickelodeon shows. The feeling was cold and resided just below my stomach. It made everything around me seem unreal and unsafe. I could most closely equate it with the sensation I felt when, at age three, I was taken to the hospital in the night with sudden hives. My parents were away, on a trip, and so my Brazilian babysitter Flavia had rushed me to the ER, where a doctor placed me on a high bed and pressed a cold stethoscope between my shoulder blades. On our way into the hospital I was sure I had seen a man sleeping inside of a mailbag. In hindsight, he must have been on a gurney, covered in a dark blanket. Maybe he was comatose or even dead. The doctor removed my shirt, checked under my armpits, and all the while I hovered above us, dissociated, observing.

This chain reaction of observations and implications would repeat itself throughout my childhood, in the face of this unnamed fear, and I came to refer to it as "hospital feeling." I decided it could be cured by taking a swig of grape juice.

I was able to put a finer point on this feeling when my

grandmother died. I was fourteen. I had recently colored my hair and bought a satin tube top, a transition I considered to be evidence of irreversible maturity. I showed up to my last visit with my grandmother in rich brown lipstick and a slim collarless coat, bought on sale at Banana Republic. I painted my dying grandmother's fingernails carefully with a pearlescent polish by Wet *n* Wild and promised to return for lunch the next day. But there was no next day: she died late that night, my father by her side. The following morning, when he recounted her passing to us, was the first and last time I saw him cry.

Until I was about twelve my grandmother was my best friend. Carol Marguerite Reynolds—Gram, as I called her—was in possession of a swirling bob of snow-white hair and only one eyebrow, a result of a lack of UV awareness. She was in the habit of drawing on the missing one with a gray-blue Maybelline pencil that didn't even begin to suggest natural hair growth. She wore pants from the maternity store to accommodate her distended belly and the kind of practical shoes that have, in recent years, become fashionable in Brooklyn. Her house smelled of mothballs, baby powder, and a loamy moistness that emanated from her overstuffed basement. I called her every day at 4:00 P.M.

On the surface, she was traditional. Provincial even. A retired real-estate agent in Old Lyme, Connecticut, with a passion for Dan Rather and a freezer full of cheap London broil, she wasn't particularly interested in our life in the city. (In fact, I only remember her visiting once, an event I was so excited for that I put out the milk for tea at 10:00 A.M., and it spoiled by her 4:00 P.M. arrival.) But the trappings of her domestic life hid what I now see was the soul of a radical. After attending a one-room schoolhouse in a town full of swamp Yankees—her family had been the first of their neighbors to have a car, which they drove across the frozen lake in winter—she had fled her sheltered life for Mount Holyoke College, Yale nursing school, and then the army, where she was stationed in Germany and Japan suturing wounds and removing shrapnel from German soldiers despite strict orders to let them die. She dated doctors (some of them Jews!) and adopted a dachshund named Meatloaf she'd found rummaging through the trash behind her tent.

Gram recounted her adventures with Plymouth Rock stoicism, but it was clear to me, even as a nine-year-old, that she'd seen far more than she was willing to discuss.

Gram didn't marry until she was thirty-four, which, in 1947, was the equivalent of being Liza Minnelli on her fifth gay husband. My grandfather, also named Carroll, was massively obese and came from great wealth, which he had squandered on a series of misguided investments including a chicken farm and a business that sold "all-in-one sporting cages." But Gram saw something in him, and within two weeks they were engaged. From this union came my father and his brother, Edward, aka Jack.

The day after Gram died, my father and I drove up to her house one last time, and I listened to Aimee Mann on a Discman and watched the industrial landscape pass by. This drive had been a fixture of my childhood: abandoned hospitals and train tracks, signs for towns that didn't live up to their names, a stop in New Haven for pizza and gas. This, I remember thinking, is the end. Nothing had ever ended before.

As my father and Uncle Jack organized Gram's things in preparation to sell her house, I wandered the halls in her bathrobe, her crumpled tissues still in the pockets, wailing. They kept working, seemingly immune to the magnitude of the occasion.

"I can't believe she saved all these fucking receipts," my father hissed. "There's canned soup in the cellar from 1965."

"She was just here!" I shouted at the unfeeling adults. "And now she's gone! Her things are still in the REFRIGERA-TOR!"

When I emerged from the bathroom smelling her comb, my uncle took my father aside and asked him to please make me stop.

Enraged by the request, I retreated to her closet and switched to sniffing her pajamas. My head throbbed with questions. Where is Gram? Is she conscious? Is she lonely? And what does this all mean for *me?*

The rest of the summer was characterized by a kind of hot terror, a lurking dread that cast a pallor over everything I did. Every ice pop I ate, every movie I watched, every poem I wrote, was tinged with a sense of impending loss. Not of another loved one but of my own life. It could be tomorrow. It could be eighty years from tomorrow. But it was coming for us all, and I was no exception.

So what were we playing at?

Finally, one day, I couldn't stand it anymore: I walked into the kitchen, laid my head on the table, and asked my father, "How are we supposed to live every day if we know we're going to die?" He looked at me, clearly pained by the dawning of my genetically predestined morbidity. He had been the same way as a kid. A day never went by where he didn't think about his eventual demise. He sighed, leaned back in his chair, unable to conjure a comforting answer. "You just do."

My father can get pretty existential. "You're born alone and you die alone" is a favorite of his that I particularly hate. Ditto "Perhaps reality is just a chip implanted in all our brains." He has a history of staring out into nature and asking, "How do we know this is actually *here?*" I guess I inherited it. I thought about Gram, about how long and complicated her life had been, and how it had now been reduced to a Dumpster full of old canned goods and a vintage Pucci sweater I had already spilled tomato sauce on. I thought about all the things I hoped to get done in my life and realized: I better get cracking. I can never spend a whole afternoon watching a *Singled Out* marathon again if *this* is what's going to happen.

· 🎸 ·

The fact is I had been circling the topic of death, subconsciously, for some time. Growing up in Soho in the late 1980s and early 1990s, I was aware of AIDS and the toll it was taking on the creative community. Illness, loss, who would handle the art and the real estate and the medical bills—these topics hovered over every dinner party. As many of my parents' friends became sick, I learned to recognize the look of someone suffering—sunken cheeks, odd facial spotting, a sweater that no longer fit. And I knew what it meant: that person would soon become a memorial, the name on a prize given to visiting students, a distant memory.

**Fig. I.**

a.

b.

Gram's bathrobe (a.) with requisite crumpled tissue (b.)

My mom's best friend, Jimmy, was a swarthy gay fetish photographer who was dying by the time I was born. One of my earliest memories is of a pale, feeble man reclining on the couch by the front windows of our loft, joking weakly with my mother about gossip, and family, and fashion. He was charismatic, talented, darkly funny. My mother helped him get his affairs in order, reached out to friends who hadn't seen him in a long time to say good-bye, navigated New York with his mother when she came to be with Jimmy in his final days. I still have a lot of guilt for screaming at Jimmy when he ate a banana I had been "saving," especially since he died a few weeks later.

Fig. 2.

The banana Jimmy stole from me.

The summer after sophomore year of college I became con-vinced I, too, would die of AIDS. I had ill-advised intercourse with a petite poet-mathematician who, afterward, removed the condom, placed it under his pil-low, and wiped his penis clean on his own curtains.

"Can I tell you a secret?" he asked as he returned to bed.

"Lay it on me!" I said.

"Well," he said, "last week I was walking around late at night and I accidentally wandered into a gay bar and I met this Filipino guy and let him come to my house, and he fucked me in the ass and the condom broke and then he stole my wallet."

I paused. "I'm so sorry that happened to you," I said.

It was about a hundred degrees out, the kind of New York heat that chafes your thighs and makes the murder rate spike. I spent the rest of the summer in a hell of my own cre-ation, imagining the virus taking hold, the things I'd never do, the children I'd never have, the tears my mother would shed as she lost yet another loved one to this pandemic. I had done enough research to know that, were I infected, it wouldn't show up on a test for several months, so I simply waited and asked myself questions: Was I strong enough to be an activist? What would it feel like to be the face of AIDS in the industrialized world? Or would I simply hide until I died? I asked to have my wisdom teeth removed, just so I could be unconscious for a few hours. I tried to enjoy every bite of Tasti D and every laugh shared with my sister, knowing things would soon change. I made out with a computer programmer and wondered if I had exposed him to the illness. By the end of the summer I was officially "living with AIDS."

Spoiler alert: I was fine.

As much as I wanted to believe the universe punishes you for fucking a minuscule bisexual, I had not contracted the virus. But the chilling specter of my own death had been so all consuming, I'd required dental surgery.

"I don't mind the idea of dying," my friend Elizabeth says, "but I'm stressed out about the logistics of the whole thing."

If we are reincarnated, as my mother promises, how long do we have to wait around before we get inside that new baby? Is it a long line, like the Japanese girls lined up outside a newly opened Topshop? What if that new baby has mean parents? If we follow the Buddhist logic that we are becoming part of the glory of the universe, one huge consciousness, well, that's just too much togetherness for my taste. I couldn't even do a group art project in second grade. How am I going to share an understanding with the rest of creation? If this proves to be the case, I'm too much of a loner for death, but I'm also scared of being lonely. Where does that leave me?

·   ♟   ·

After reading an early version of this essay, my friend Matt asked me: "Why are you in such a rush to die?" I was shocked by the question, even a little pissed. This wasn't about me! This was about the universal plight, which I happen to have an exceptionally clear perspective on because of my inability to ignore it like some other nincompoops!

I had never thought of it that way, but Matt was right. The hypochondria. The intensity of my reactions to death, and my inability to disengage with the topic once it is raised in a group. My need to make it clear to everyone that it's coming for them, too. My need to meditate on it. Is what's manifesting as a fear actually some instinct to resist being young? Youth, with all its accompanying risks, humiliations, and uncertainties, the pressure to do it all before it's too late. Is the sense of imminent death bound up in the desire to leave some kind of a legacy? I did once write, though never shot, a short film in which I held a massive funeral, heard everyone I love speak on the topic of me, then jumped out of my casket at the end and yelled, "Surprise!"

I am still in my twenties so a fear of death is, while reasonable in a macro way, also fairly irrational. Most people live through their twenties. And their thirties. And their forties. Many people live longer than is amusing, even to them. So every time I think about death, when I lie in bed and imagine

Fig. 3.

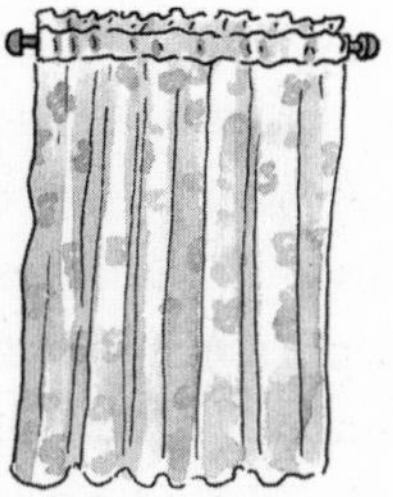

The curtain my date wiped his dick on.

disintegrating, my skin going leathery and my hair petrifying and a tree growing out of my stomach, it's a way to avoid what's right in front of me. It's a way to not be here, in the uncertainty of right now.

If I live long enough and am given a chance to read this when I'm old, I'll probably be appalled at my own audacity to think that I have any sense of what death means, what it brings to light, what it feels like to live with the knowledge that it is coming. How could someone whose biggest health scare was a coffee-induced colon infection know what the end of life looks like? How could someone who has never lost a parent, a lover, or a best friend have the faintest clue about what any of this means?

My dad, who looks pretty great for sixty-four, is fond of saying, "You just can't fucking imagine, Lena." He can see the big event in the distance (his belief in robotics not withstanding) and says things like "Bring it on. At this point, I'm fucking curious." I get it: I know nothing. But I also hope that future me will be proud of present me for trying to wrap my head around the big ideas and also for trying to make you feel like we're all in this together.

Gram's sister is still alive.* Doad is one hundred, with the energy of someone in her early eighties. Although her body resists most activity, she still knits, whittles, and practices the organ. She has the kind of Yankee disposition that takes things as they come. For her, cancer is akin to a shopping center going up next door: inconvenient and unexpected,

---

* Doris Reynolds Jewett died peacefully on December 10, 2013, having very recently drunk a martini.

but there's not much you can do about it. She has never listened to Deepak Chopra, switched to almond milk, or medi-
tated. Yet she is here, in the chair by the window in the house
she was born in, outliving her husband and siblings and
nephews and friends.

My father and I visit her about once a year. I ask her about
her thoughts on current events ("Obama seems like a nice
kid and handsome to boot") and the history of her house
("One toilet and five kids; it was a goddamn joke"). She uses
the expression "not in a dog's age!" the way millennials say
"like." My father, when beholding a woman with the same
matter-of-fact staccato and cap of white hair as his mother,
becomes withdrawn, childlike. He shuffles his feet the same
way he does at his mother's grave or in traffic court, all traces
of radicalism gone.

Doad wrote a memoir. Seventeen years ago, when she was
already pretty damn old. She chronicled life in her town in
the early part of the twentieth century—the first car, the first
television, the first divorce. She wrote about the one-room
schoolhouse, her lone black friend, and the time her brother
climbed on a ladder in a devil mask, peered into her bedroom window, and scared her so badly she wet herself. She
did it not for glory but for posterity—spare, practical prose
designed simply to get the information out, to prove that she
was there and that she is still here. She's proud of the fact
that, at her age, she doesn't need help to dress—plaid shirt,
nurse's shoes, pastel "dungarees."

The last time we visit, she gives us a pile of scarves she
knit by hand, all slightly too short, the stitches uneven and
lumpy. When we leave she says we didn't stay long enough,
and we promise we'll be back, next time with my sister. We
hug goodbye, and I can feel the curve of her spine, each ver-
tebra bulging.

On the ride back to the city, my father and I encounter some of the "most hideous" traffic he has ever seen. We creep along the highway, and he relaxes his grip on the wheel, grows contemplative. "We should visit Doad more," he says. "She knows we only stay for forty-five minutes. She's not senile."

I try something new out on him, something I've been thinking, or wondering whether I think: "I'm really not afraid to die," I say. "Not anymore. Something's changed."

"Well," he says, "I'm sure your feelings about that will continue to evolve as you get older. As you see more death around you and things happen to your body. But I hope you always feel that way."

I know he loves talking about death. It just takes him a second to get warmed up.

"You know," he says. "It just can't be a bad thing. Because it's everything."

We talk about enlightened beings, what it would mean to transcend the human plane. "I want to be enlightened, but it also sounds boring," I tell him. "So much of what I love—gossip and furniture and food and the Internet—are really here, on earth." Then I say something that would probably make the Buddha roll over in his grave: "I think I could be enlightened, but I'm not in the mood yet. I just want to work the death thing out."

We crest a hill in the wet dark and see, before us, a string of cars, lit up red, at a standstill as far as the eye can see. We are hours from home. "Holy shit," he says. "That is fucking insane. Is this even real?"

# *My Top 10 Health Concerns*

**1.** We are all afraid of cancer. From what I understand it's a threat that is always just looming inside your body, but isn't a problem until it is. It could be living anywhere from your liver to that adorable signature mole on your hip, and it could either kill you or spark a memoir. I'm not scared enough to do any 10K walks, but I'm pretty scared.

**2.** I think a lot about chronic fatigue syndrome. Its symptoms sound awful, like a flu that will never ever end, that drains you and makes you an exhausting burden on your family and friends until you finally are just an idea of a person. (I am sure medical authorities and sufferers alike will love this description.) It gets worse: some doctors think it's a mental health issue and its sufferers are delusional depressives. Other people suspect it's linked to mono, which I once had so badly that I was too tired to crumple my face when I cried. Throughout the day I often ask myself, Could I fall asleep right now? and the answer is always a resounding yes.

**3.** I'm concerned that if I ate differently, more vegetables or less toast with butter and salt, I'd feel this insane burst of energy I can only begin to imagine. That a better, stronger, more productive me exists if I would take proper steps to change my life. Even when presented with evidence of my own productivity I think that the people accusing me of being productive don't know how hard it is for me to just bend my elbow sometimes. A connected fear is that if I lost twenty pounds I'd realize I've been going through life with a backpack of fat strapped to me and I'd be able to do cartwheels and things. That being said, a homeopathic doctor once told me that we need butter to "lubricate our synapses" and the reason the divorce rate in Hollywood is so high is because everyone is underlubricated.

**4.** Related: I am scared about what my cell phone is doing to my brain. And yet I have never used an earbud for more than half a day. The most terrifying aspect of human health is our refusal to take steps to help ourselves and the fact that we are so often responsible for our own demise through lack of positive action. It makes me want to take a nap.

**5.** Tonsil stones. Do you know about tonsil stones? Well, let me ask you this: Have you ever coughed up a small white rock that, upon further inspection, smelled like the worst corners of the New York sewer system? If so, I'm sure you were shocked this came from your own body and you flushed it away and hoped never to think of it again. That was a tonsil stone. They form in the crypts of your tonsils, where food and dead skin and various detritus collect and ferment, creating the most disgusting thing your body is capable of producing (and that's saying a lot). In addition to their unseemliness, they are also a source of infection and discomfort. I myself have the occasional stone and asked my doctor to inspect my tonsils, which he described as "teeming balls of disease." And yet, when I asked about removing them, he seemed unconcerned. He said I would have to rest for two weeks and would lose at least fifteen pounds, which is not the way to deter me. How, I ask, can it be even remotely okay to have this happening in one's throat? Will other people sense it and, in an apocalyptic situation, leave me behind to choke on my stones and die?

**6.** I live in fear of tinnitus. A constant ringing in my ear that will drive me mad, that will keep me awake and interrupt my conversations and even when it's cured I'll still hear its malevolent harmony. If I lie very still at night I can fully imagine it, a sound like a bug being boiled to death.

**7.** I am very scared of lamp dust. I have a serious problem with dust coming out of my lamps. Everything I put under my lamps is, within minutes, covered in a thick layer of dust. In related news, my left nostril is never not clogged, and once the ear, nose, and throat doctor sucked all the mucus out of my sinuses with a tiny vacuum and for three hours I felt a 45 percent spike in my quality of life until it refilled again.

**8.** I'm afraid of adrenal fatigue. This is related to chronic fatigue but not the same. Western doctors don't believe in adrenal fatigue, but if you have a job and are a human, then any holistic doctor will tell you that you have adrenal fatigue. It is essentially a dangerous exhaustion that comes from ambition and modern life. I have it so bad. Please read about it on the Internet—you do, too.

**9.** The surface of my tongue is insane. It looks like a cartoon of the moon. It just can't be right.

**10.** I'm afraid that I am infertile. My uterus *does* tilt to the right, which could mean it's an inhospitable environment for a child who wants a straight-down-the-line kind of uterus. And so I will adopt, but I won't have the sort of beautiful, genetics-defying love story that *People* magazine chronicles. The kid will have undiagnosed fetal alcohol syndrome. He will hate me, and he will nail our dog to a board.

# *Hello Mother, Hello Father*
## *Greetings from Fernwood Cove Camp for Girls*

MY MOTHER AND GRANDMOTHER attended "green-and-white" camp. That was their shorthand for a respectable summer home for privileged Jewish girls whose parents were away on cruises, where the uniform consisted of crisp green shorts and a collared white shirt.

They described camp, which they attended for eight weeks every summer from ages six to seventeen, as a sort of utopia for little girls. Nestled deep in the woods of southern Maine, you roasted marshmallows and traded secrets and learned to use a bow and arrow. Even my mother, a teenager so sullen and ornery that she refused to eat dinner with her family, came alive at camp. At home she was angry, disgusted by her father's vaudeville sense of humor and her mother's careful attention to social mores. She hated her blond sisters' attempts to fit in socially and her maid for needing money badly enough to leave her own family. But at camp she had a bunk of sisters, girls who understood her, girls who she waited all through the freezing, lonely winter to see. At camp she was able to express an enthusiasm and passion she never let her family witness. And when the summer ended, she was heartbroken.

When I was little I would lie in bed, drifting off as my mother told me tales: of color wars, canoe trips, and pranks galore. Of the camp mother, who roughly shampooed your head once a week and set your hair in curlers. Of undying friendship, a world where youth ruled and boys could not disturb the idyll. In my mind her camp stories have mingled irrevocably with the plot of *The Parent Trap,* lending my image of her long-ago summers a Technicolor flair.

When I was ten, we took a road trip to Maine to visit family friends and made a stop at the now-abandoned Camp Weno-nah. From the passenger side I could see empty cabins, a tennis court with the net slumping toward the ground. My mother sprang out of the car with the same manic excite-ment that she must have felt every summer when her parents dropped her off. She's been five-foot-ten since she was thir-teen or fourteen, and I could just picture that same lanky body bounding out of bed in time for the morning salute and flag raising.

Now, nearing fifty and wearing the kind of straw hat that makes me want to kill myself, she walked us over a grassy hill to reveal a gray lake vista, forgotten wooden boats knocking against the shore. On this exact spot, she told us, was where they held the outdoor mixers with neighboring boys camp Skylamar. Over there, she thought, was the arts-and-crafts cabin, now just a husk of its former self. And suddenly, she was crying. I'd never seen her cry before and I stared, unsure of my next move.

"Stop looking at me," she snapped. "I'm not a science experiment."

I asked if she still spoke to any of her Wenonah friends. No, she said, but that didn't mean she'd ever stop loving them—they were sisters.

So I wanted camp, too. I didn't want to leave home. I loved my loft bed and my hairless cat and the small desk my father had installed for me in what used to be the closet where he kept his sci-fi paperbacks. I loved our mint-green elevator and our Malaysian takeout and August in New York, the way the only breeze came from the subway rushing past. But I also wanted friendships, fresh starts with people who had never seen me wet myself during Wiffle ball or hit my father outside the deli. I wanted memories so powerful they made you cry. And by God, I wanted green shorts.

I spent three summers at Fernwood Cove Camp for Girls.

Fernwood Cove was the sister camp of Fernwood, a long-standing institution that Wenonah had regularly opposed in sports. Fernwood Cove was for four-weekers, girls too scared to spend eight weeks away from home. Or too spoiled to live without electricity. Or too slutty to live without boys. I had decided eight weeks was too much for me when my cousin, a Fernwood girl, described the ritualistic beheading of a weakling's stuffed animal. "I mean, you just don't bring a *toy* to camp," she said, like it was obvious.

I started at Fernwood Cove when I was thirteen. I had just finished a successful seventh-grade year in which I had enjoyed not one but *two* popular boyfriends and gotten my hair highlighted by a licensed beautician named Beata. This rare winning streak was only slightly dampened by the short bangs

I had cut myself in order to prepare for my audition as Drew Barrymore's little sister in the Penny Marshall film *Riding in Cars with Boys*. (The role went to someone else after I told Ms. Marshall I could not smile on command. "That's called *acting*," she growled.)

So it was with a rare sense of hope and anticipation that I boarded the bus in Boston that would take me to Fernwood Cove. On the three-hour drive I got to know my seatmate, a girl named Lydia Green Hamburger, who told me, within three minutes of meeting me, that she knew Lindsay Lohan. Lydia was different from me—she talked animatedly about school dances and lacrosse and the mall—and yet we got along handsomely. This is what camp is all about! I thought. Meeting other, slightly different kinds of white girls!

But the moment we pulled into the dusty driveway and I saw the tetherball waiting, the fear set in.

If my behavior that first summer at camp was the only evidence a psychiatrist had to go on, they would have diagnosed me as a fast-cycling bipolar. My emotions vacillated wildly, from joy to despair to disdain of my fellow campers. One minute I was passionately engaged with my new friend Katie, and the next I was convinced she had the IQ of a lima bean. One minute I was reveling in the moment, not thinking about my family at all, and the next, walking from the rock wall to the drama tent, I would be hit with a wave of homesickness so severe I was sure I would die right then and there. My parents seemed impossibly far away—dead, for all I knew. That sense became harder to shake, and as the summer progressed my homesickness only grew more intense, which was the exact opposite of what my father had promised me would happen.

The only thing that distracted me fully was being allowed to present a play I had written about a woman with thirteen cats who was searching for an understanding mate. On the strength of this work, my drama counselor Rita-Lynn cast me as the star of a play she'd written about "primal coyote women" for her thesis at Yale drama school. I was thrilled until I learned I would have to drop a potato from between my legs and grunt, "Uh, what a good poop." How could they ask a serious actor to deliver such an absurd phrase!?

But when the line got a laugh at dress rehearsal, I decided it was genius.

I was in hell. I was in heaven. I was at camp.

·  ▶  ·

There were ten of us, living in a three-hundred-square-foot bunk, going through puberty at lightning speed. It was too much hormonal action for any one room, and the result was a frenzied, emotionally volatile space that smelled like a Bath and Body Works.

Just because there weren't boys at camp doesn't mean there wasn't romance. We had socials—two per summer, just like my mother did at Wenonah—and we prepared, laying our outfits out a week in advance, trading sandy tubes of lip gloss and glow-in-the-dark barrettes.

My new friend Ashley, a sporty blonde who was dating the heir to the Utz potato chip fortune, lent me a neon tube top and twisted my hair into tiny fashion dreadlocks. As I returned the favor, applying blush to her already rosy cheeks, I noticed something: "You have an eyelash," I told her, and brushed it away, only to realize the long black hair was actually growing out of her cheek.

We were all in various stages of puberty. Charlotte had full-scale breasts, so big that they hung down, casting a half-moon shadow on her rib cage. Marianna seemed unaware she was growing hair in her armpits, or maybe they didn't care in Colombia, where she was from. I was flat as a board, hairless too, and fine with it, but I couldn't stop eying everyone else, staring at their round asses as they dressed, the dusky hairs emerging from their bathing suits. "You are so bicurious!" my counselor Liz shrieked at me when she caught me watching her tits swing as she changed.

My greatest obsession was BO. I smelled it everywhere: in the bathroom, on the wind during kickball, on Emily's hairbrush, which I borrowed because my old one was growing some kind of mold. I couldn't imagine a life where that smell, just enough like onions to be truly confusing, came from your own body. Then one afternoon, sitting on my own bed at rest hour, I swore I smelled it. Not too strong, but there, on my t-shirt. A bit of research led me to an area near my right armpit. *I got it from hugging Charlotte,* I thought. In fact, I was sure of it. I wrote home immediately, explaining the whole dreadful situation. "How do I tell Charlotte without being mean?" I asked.

In a letter back, my father gently explained that BO was hard to transfer and that, just to be safe, I might want to ask for a natural antiperspirant on the next run to Walmart.

The first social of the summer took place at Camp Skylamar, a forty-minute drive from Fernwood Cove, in a barn full of pimply boys in short-sleeved button-downs and boat shoes. *NSYNC and Brandy played on a weak stereo system. The girls danced nervously in a cluster while the boys hung around the edges of the room pounding fruit punch. At some point in the night, I opened the door to the bathroom to find a boy hunched over the toilet, furiously masturbating.

After dusk, I fell into conversation with a fourteen-year-old from New Jersey named Brent. He was handsome, with a baseball hat and a boxer's flat face. I told him I went to school in Brooklyn and he said he didn't know where that was because he wasn't "so good at geometry." After the longest twenty minutes in history, he asked me if I'd like to come to the back porch with him, which I understood was code for mashing our beaks together like baby birds.

"I'm sorry, but I don't feel we know each other well enough," I told him. "But if you want my address, you can have it, and we can see what develops."

As I left, Emily said she saw him give me the finger behind my back.

All night at Skylamar I'd had this uncanny sense of recognition, like déjà vu but unceasing. I had been there before, knew the contours of the place; the bunks dotted the hill in a familiar way. The cafeteria building welcomed me. And as I lay in bed that night, I realized: this was Wenonah. Skylamar was built on the site where my mother's camp had once stood.

This was the place that my mother had called home for ten summers, where she had met the women who were still sisters to her today despite the geography and ideologies that divide them. This was where she had played Rhett Butler on the summer stage, been introduced to the joys of instant macaroni and cheese, and contracted a case of lice that necessitated cutting her hair into a jagged bob. This is where her parents left her when they decided to take a seven-week boat trip around Europe, wearing their finest hats.

After my first summer at Fernwood Cove, it seemed pretty obvious to my parents that I would not return. Despite moments of pleasure, I had sobbed hysterically on every phone call home, wailing, "Please come get me. I'm begging you." I felt ganged up on by my bunkmates and misunderstood by my counselors. I had developed an "allergy to wood."

I was a quitter: of play dates, of dance class, of Hebrew school. Nothing in my history indicated I would stick it out. But when December's enrollment deadline rolled around, I shocked my parents (and myself): "I think I want to give camp another try."

"Are you sure?" my father asked. "You didn't seem happy."

"No, you didn't," my mother agreed. "You can do day camp. Or no camp."

"I'm sure," I said. "I think it's important."

Some of my camp memories actually belong to my mother. Certain images, though vivid to me, are from stories she told me in bed. For example, I never roasted dough on a stick and then filled the hole left by the stick with butter and jam. That was her. I never caught two female counselors kissing on the archery range, pressed against a target, one's hand down the other's shorts. When the boys came to Wenonah for a social they canoed across the lake, arriving at dusk like an enemy tribe, storming the shore in tiny blazers. And although the boys showed up at our camp in a bunch of church vans, I can still see them tying up their boats and spilling over the hill ready to pillage us.

Sometimes I will find myself telling one of these stories to a group: the time I saw two lesbians in action. The best snack to make over a fire. It takes me a second to realize that I am lying. My best memories, the ones I hold dearest from my time at Fernwood Cove, aren't mine at all. They belong to someone else. My stories are terrible. No one will be as excited to hear about me hiding in the bathroom to take my OCD medication. The time I stayed home from a field trip with a fake migraine isn't a nostalgic crowd pleaser. Diarrhea in a canyon during a lengthy hike isn't right for every audience. I can't remember any of the songs.

· ✦ ·

In keeping with my life at home in New York, my "true friends" at camp were adult staff members.

The counselors were a diverse group, utterly suitable for an early season of *The Real World*. Girls with belly-button rings and ankle tattoos. Mormon guys in wifebeaters who listened to gangster rap. Even the fat ones had hard, tan legs. They seemed completely under one another's spells, seduced by their own youth and beauty. This became clear when, from the window of my top bunk, I saw their wide white asses cavorting on the dock past midnight when they were supposed to be *guarding our lives*.

The first summer I lusted after a college student named Buddhu Bengay, who was from Western Mass and wore rope sandals like Jesus Christ himself. He had acne scarring and monstrous big toes but the way he talked reminded me of Matthew Perry, so dry that even regular words seemed funny. We only spoke a few times, though during a kitchen raid he did once pick me up and carry me back to my bunk. I beat his chest, stunned that he was touching me. He smelled like deodorant, the real kind, not the organic stuff my father wore.

"No way, young lady," he said as he deposited me on the porch of Bunk Kingfisher. My legs shook, like I was stepping onto land for the first time in weeks.

I also flirted with an attraction to Rocco, my Australian "bunk uncle," who claimed to be having a fling with Diana Ross's daughter, the improbably named Chudney. Though the male counselors were not allowed to enter our bunks without at least two female counselors present, Rocco would often sit outside the screen door and talk to us as the sun went down after dinner. He called me Dunny, which, he explained, was Aussie slang for "toilet."

But I found my truest love during my second summer, and his name was Johnny. Johnny McDuff. He was blond, from South Carolina, and just shy of twenty-two. He dressed in Dickies and Morrissey t-shirts and Wayfarers. He played guitar, songs he'd written himself with titles like "Oogie Boogie Girl" and "Angel Watchin' over Me," walked into the dining room late, with the easy swagger of a first-born child. People said he had a crush on Kelsey the crafts counselor, but I didn't believe it. She wore a hemp anklet. She lay out to tan. She was common.

Johnny accompanied us on a number of field trips. It was under his watchful eye that we rode bumper cars, saw *I Know What You Did Last Summer*, camped in a trailer park where I heard a man scream "I'm fuckin' done witchu" to his wife and speed off into the darkness on his motorcycle. We went whitewater rafting with a guide named Bear who taught me the term "AMFYOYO" (an acronym for "adios motherfucker, you're on your own"). And we drove four hours to a forty-foot cliff with the intention of jumping off of it.

On the way there, I decided I was going to jump first. It was a silent decision. My skills as a camper were undeveloped to say the least. I remained afraid of the dark. I won an award for "worst bed maker." I had gotten across the ropes course exactly once, with help. Sometimes Karen and Jojo played a game where they pushed me to the ground then timed how long it took me to get up before pushing me down again. Jumping first, before the rest of my bunkmates, would be a strong move to the basket, a way to reverse my position as the weakest and whiniest member of Kingfisher. As the other girls hemmed and hawed and pretended to be scared, I would step to the edge and dive effortlessly into the water, slicing the surface with my hands slightly cupped—just like our diving instructor had taught us.

As we neared the site in the van, I couldn't contain myself. "I'm jumping the second we get there," I announced.

"Yeah, right," Jojo said.

As the other girls set up their towels and adjusted their Speedo two-pieces, I approached the edge of the cliff. Holy fucking shit, it was high. The kind of height that makes your insides turn to jelly.

"It's a long way down, isn't it?" There was Johnny, right behind me. He was pink and sunburned in little blue shorts. He looked like a World War II soldier on furlough.

"I'm cold," I said. "I want to wait a second."

"It's not gonna get any easier," he said.

"I know. I might not go at all," I told him, starting back toward the other girls. I was ready to be mocked. I didn't care, just as long as I was far away from that cliff. It goes against nature to hurl yourself off a giant rock into a pool of murky water.

"I tell you what, I'll go with you."

Nearly fifteen years later, my body goes wild just writing this. I looked at Johnny.

"Really?"

He nodded. "Hell, yeah."

"Count," I said.

"Okay." He nodded, stepping past me, a little closer to the edge. "I'm going to start now. Ready? One . . . two . . ."

And we jumped. It wasn't the clean dive I had pictured. I panicked and wriggled in the air like a new kitten, trying to claw my way back up again. Before I could process the sensation of falling I had hit the water, hard and at the wrong angle. The cold soothed the hurt soothed the fear. Johnny landed a moment later and when we surfaced, me sputtering and coughing, yanking my bathing suit out of my butt crack, he nodded a relaxed congratulations, flipping his yellow hair out of his eyes.

Later that afternoon, when we stopped for some roadside ice cream, he asked to taste my flavor, bubblegum. He wrapped his tongue around my cone—in my memory it's an impossibly thick, red tongue—and my insides felt even weirder than they had during the jump. I knew he was sending me a secret signal. We could play along, we could have fun with the group, but we were too much for this place.

That night in my bunk, I imagined shedding my clothes, approaching Johnny, and letting him put his hands all over my body. Maybe we would meet outside, in a tent, down the path in the woods. I was practical enough to imagine that he would bring the condom.

· 🐱 ·

Our last summer, as privileged seniors, we took a bunk trip to New Hampshire to hike, camp, and see a movie. The trip was chaperoned by Rita-Lynn, Cheryl, and Rocco, and it was impossible to tell who had a crush on who in the threesome. As fifteen-year-old campers, we vaguely resembled adults, and the vibe of the trip was distinctly collegial, the counselors addressing us like knowing peers. They barely had to assert their authority and we amused ourselves, gossiping in the back of the van, journaling and singing Britney Spears songs at the top of our lungs.

On the last night of the trip it rained and, using a camp credit card, our counselors checked us into a motel. We all gathered in Rita-Lynn's room to play cards and eat peanut butter and jelly and I noticed, out of the corner of my eye, Rocco opening a beer. And another. And another. He passed one to Rita. One to Cheryl. Took a swig of his own.

I got up and motioned to Rita to join me in the bathroom. "Can I talk to you a minute?" I asked.

"What's up?" she asked. "Need a tampon?"

"No. I wanted to say that I'm not really comfortable having the only adults who are with us drinking *alcohol.*"

She looked at me blankly.

"Several people in my family have issues with alcohol abuse so it brings up a lot for me," I tried.

"Dude." She looked down at her Tevas. It was unclear whether she was frustrated or guilty. "I really thought you'd be cool."

On the last night of camp we all wore white and the seniors sent candles out into the lake on tiny rafts and sang "I Will Remember You" by Sarah McLachlan. Everyone sobbed and clutched at one another, making promises to write, to never forget. I cried, too, wishing the whole thing could have been different, that I could have been different. I stared at my candle until my eyes crossed and it disappeared into the dark.

Recently, I awoke from a camp dream so vivid it haunted me the whole next day. I was back at Fernwood Cove, and I had one last summer to make it count. Our bunk was still intact, and so was my hymen. I wasn't focused on any guy, or on writing home. We were all there, all us girls, and we loved one another dearly.

In this dream I had long, long hair, full of feathers and beads, and I was naked on the dock. My body was longer, more limber, more like my mother's. I dove backward into the water, landing perfectly without disturbing the surface.

# My Regrets

ONE DAY AT CAMP there was a field trip for the soccer team, so everyone in my bunk cleared out except me.

Being alone—without the drone of midwestern accents, without the rustle of hair braiding or the slap of shower shoes—was so delicious. I decided to skip my waterskiing class and write letters and nap. And anyway, what was the point? I never even got a real turn. There were too many of us in the class, so mostly we just shivered on the dock in our life jackets, listening to Claire B. cry because her father was turning ninety.

But the few times I did get on skis, I found the experience otherworldly: I flew. Sometimes for mere seconds, but once it was minutes. Three at least. The world sped by: boats and houses and what looked like sketches of pine trees. Until I hit a choppy patch and, inexperienced as I was, wiped out hard. Skis flew, I did splits that weren't natural to me, and I hit the surface ass first, nostrils second.

I woke up at sunset, hot and itchy, to the sound of my bunkmates returning home high on victory. "We smoked 'em!" Madeleine shouted, hurling her dirty socks into my lower bunk.

"They were slow and faaat," Emily squealed, stripping down to her sports bra.

"Sooo suu-pair coo-elll," Phillipine added in broken English, her dumb French face demented with pride.

At bonfire the waterskiing counselor asked me where I'd been. "Everyone else was on the field trip. You would have had the whole hour all to yourself."

Can you imagine what my life would be like now if that had happened?

# *Guide to Running Away*

## A GUIDE TO RUNNING AWAY
## FOR NINE-YEAR-OLD GIRLS

You want to run away. You want to run away for a lot of reasons, but let's start with the most immediate: you are mad. At your father, because he's not taking you seriously when you say you think you'll lose your mind if you have to spend another night in your bedroom alone, staring at the moon. He thinks you're having kid problems. He thinks kids have to "get through" their kid problems. He says, "just try and understand that it won't get worse. The worst that will happen is it will stay the same." This doesn't comfort you. Because he doesn't know there's something in you—big, explosive, ready to surprise the world in a bad way if you're not handled right, but ready to be beautiful if someone will just listen.

You are mad at your mother because sometimes she doesn't pay attention and she says yes to a question that needs a different kind of answer. She is distracted. When she holds your hand it's too loose and you have to show her how to do it right, how to make a little hammock for your fingers. You are mad at your mother because she's sitting on the porch in her capri pants, talking on the telephone, telling someone else that you're having a good summer.

You are mad to be spending the summer in the country, where the days are too quiet and you have so much time to think. In the city you live on Broadway, where the noise is so thick your scary thoughts can't get a word in edgewise. But here in the country, there is only space. On the stone bridge by the stream. On the mossy rock at the edge of the yard. Behind the abandoned trailer where Art, the old man with the glass eye, used to live. Space, space, space, and you can scare yourself into thinking your thoughts are more like voices.

Your godparents, also city people, live a mile down the road. She has red hair and cat's-eye glasses; he is bald and does one voice to impersonate all four Beatles. One day your godfather and you get on your cordless phones and leave the house and see if you can make it to each other before they go static. You see him crest the hill, waving, just as his voice crackles and disintegrates.

Last week your parents had a party. Everyone drove up from the city. Artists, writers, boyfriends, girlfriends, a woman with purple eyebrows, and they parked their cars all across your lawn. Gregory's brother made wine out of lilacs, and you took three sips, then pretended to be drunk, making a big show out of being unable to walk a straight line, like a drunk person on *I Love Lucy*. Around ten your parents sent you up to your room and you listened to the party burn down like a cigarette, your little sister breathing beside you, a trusty machine.

The day of the party had been the worst one of the summer. Your parents asked you to do chores that didn't seem fair, didn't seem like your problem, so you went to the attic and you threw raw eggs down at the front walk. Your father didn't even seem angry, just put you to work scrubbing the stone with a kitchen sponge.

The day after the party it was all about cleaning up. And the day after that it was all about doing work. And the day after that was just another day and everyone's making you sleep in your bed.

So now it's time to run away.

First, you have to pack a bag. It's probably best to use a mini backpack, so as not to weigh yourself down. You need to be able to move. You can use the baby-blue one you bought so you could feel more like Cher Horowitz in *Clueless*. But then you insisted on wearing it during dodgeball on the first day of school, and you became the fourth grade's most hunted target. Nice one, weirdo.

In terms of packing, all you need is clean underwear and a loaf of bread.

If you were running away from your city house, it'd be easy. You'd just go to the lobby and sit underneath the row of mailboxes. Remember when your hairless cat took the elevator down all on his own and hid inside the slot where Victor Carnuccio's packages go? That was so funny.

If you were scared in the lobby, watching lower Broadway pass, you wouldn't need to be. Your mother would come down soon enough and cotton to your demands.

But you're at your country house so it's a little bit harder.

A good place to hide might be: out back, behind Art's trailer. You could also go around the side of the old church, but it smells damp and is at least a quarter of a mile farther, and you hate walking.

A nice person to bring with you, should you want a companion, would be your neighbor Joseph Cranbrook. He is a good kid, even though he acts crazy sometimes. (Like when he ripped your screen door off the hinges because you wouldn't come out to play with him. Your dad talked to him like he was an adult who had made a mistake, which is how he always talks to kids and which is part of why you are running away.) Joseph may be chubby and sloppy now, his face always covered in barbecue sauce and his only virtues being that he owns a dinghy and had the idea to dress as a gorilla in suspenders for Halloween, but be forewarned that, ten years from now, he will still be short, but he will also be ripped, and he will join the air force as an outlet for his rage and you will run into him on Crosby Street your freshman year of college and he will be the first person you give a blow job to. You won't finish, just administer one horrified lick, and he won't talk to you again. He will turn out to be "engaged" to a girl name Ellie who is a good foot taller than he and lives in South Carolina. Something called Facebook will be invented where you can learn all of this.

When you run away, the point is not to escape. You aren't actually trying to disappear. You just want to attract your mother. The great fantasy is that she's somewhere, watching, like the mother in *Runaway Bunny* who becomes the tree, then becomes the lake, then becomes the moon. Your mother becomes the mini backpack and becomes the loaf of bread and becomes the bed with the Devon Sawa poster above it where you go to sulk after it's all over. She knows. *She knows.*

And eventually she comes and you get the kind of attention you've been asking for when you hang around watching her talk on the cordless and flip through the J.Crew catalog circling things with a ballpoint pen. She says she understands, that once when she was your age she hid in a garbage can for an hour, but no one came for her except her father's dental nurse.

Later in the summer your grandfather dies, and you're secretly glad. You have a place to put all your sorrow now, one that people will understand. You ride your sister's tricycle back and forth on the porch, loving the sound it makes as it scrapes the lead paint from the floor. Your parents don't believe you that it's lead paint so you ask them to drive you to the hardware store, where you purchase a small kit to test it with. The kit contains a small tube, like a lipstick, with a spongy white tip that you drag across the area you suspect of being toxic. Then you wait, and if there's lead in the paint the white will turn bright red. The test results come up negative, just gray from the dirt of the porch floor, and you are disappointed.

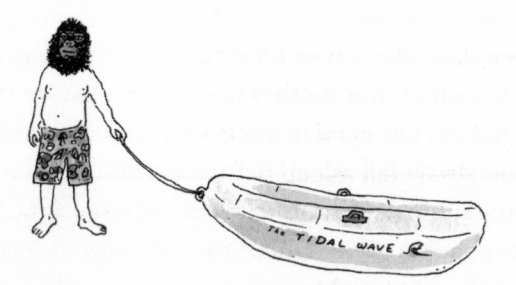

## A GUIDE TO RUNNING AWAY
## FOR TWENTY-SEVEN-YEAR-OLD WOMEN

None of your neighbors know you, so none of them would care. They are all over eighty-five, and they *don't* have HBO.

You could hurl yourself down the garbage chute and be found six days later, bleeding out into a pile of adult diapers, and it wouldn't elicit more than a "Huh?" followed by a co-op meeting on how to handle disposing of the body.

If you don't call your parents for a day, they assume you're busy at work, helping a friend recover from a minor medical procedure, or fucking your boyfriend for seventeen hours straight. An hour squatting behind a religious structure won't cut it anymore when it comes to getting their attention.

Remember when you discovered your father owned a book called *How to Disappear and Never Be Found*? You're sure it was just research for new and creative ways of thinking, for concepts that might apply to his work, but it raised the distinct possibility that there is something very upsetting that people you love could do instead of dying. You already knew your father was morbid but assumed he was as happy as he was constitutionally capable of being, and that was some comfort. That this suggests otherwise is something you would rather not focus on.

These days, the tables have turned. You're the one who's distracted while your mother tries to talk. You're the one who thinks fathers just need to get through their father problems. Now you always fall asleep before your little sister—you drop her at the subway stop and watch her disappear belowground. You hear she's a great dancer from friends who run into her when she's out at night.

You've always suffered from dissociation. Whether it's clinical, as has been suggested by at least two therapists, or willful ("Are you listening to me?" your father is always saying. "I can feel you dissociating again."), you can't say, but that syrupy terror that characterized summer nights as a nine-year-old sometimes lasts for days now.

"You know that thing, when you're having sex, but instead of feeling it you can see yourself from above, like you're watching a movie?" you ask your friend Jemima one day as she's painting you nude on her couch.

"Uh, no," she says. "And that's really sad. Have you talked to anyone about that?"

Everyone tells you that you look like your aunt. You have the same nose, the same butt, and you hug the same way, like an overcompensating koala. One day she tells you a story about when she was first dating her husband. She knew she wasn't his only girlfriend, but she liked him anyway. One evening he went out to get beer and, when she heard him return, she pretended to be asleep. Just to see what he would do. Would he cover her with a blanket? Would he walk around like she wasn't there, make an important phone call? Would he watch her sleep?

You think this must run in the family. You tried this just last week, with the person you are dating, and the results were disappointing.

The fact is, since that first blow job, you haven't gotten any more comfortable with sex. Every sexual encounter has felt like a first visit with a new general practitioner. Awkward, burdensome, a little chilly. Eventually you learn some buzzwords and positions that make the whole thing flow more easily, and you always go into it with the best intentions of not watching yourself from the doorframe like a not-very-incognito detective.

But you are still running away.

One version of running away is to take a very long shower while someone you're pretending to like sits on their bed watching trailers on the computer.

Another version is getting a UTI and, after hours of strained urination in a bathroom the size of a bucket, you slip out wearing just your nightgown, back to your parents' apartment, where your mother has set out antibiotics and cranberry juice but has gone back to bed.

Another version is calling a cab in a haze of pills and getting home at 6:00 A.M. only to realize you've left all your valuables at the home of a guy who doesn't wake up until two and can't be summoned from his narcotic sleep by the buzzer.

Another version is sneaking off to meditate in the morning, then getting back into bed like you never slipped out. Another version is just meditating.

Other things you can try: Saying you're sick. Saying you fell down in the street because of impractical shoes. Saying work ran late. Writing your head off. Saying you're sick again. Saying you're a person who gets sick a lot. Going radio silent, then saying you lost your cell phone somewhere in your bed. Going to work and staying there all day long. Listening to a Taylor Swift song about dancing in the rain. Not jogging. Never jogging.

Soon you will find yourself in more and more situations you don't want to run from. At work you'll realize that you've spent the entire day in your body, really in it, not imagining what you look like to the people who surround you but just being who you are. You are a tool being put to its proper use. That changes a lot of things.

And one day you'll get out of bed to pee, and someone will say, "I hate it when you leave," and you will *want* to rush back. You'll think, Stuff like this only happens to characters played by Jennifer Garner, right? but it's happening to you and it keeps happening even when you cry or misbehave or show him how terrible you are at planning festive group outings. He seems to be there without reservation. He pays attention. He listens. He seems to want to stay.

Sometimes that old feeling slips back in. Of being invaded

and misunderstood. Of being outside your body but still in the room, like what you imagine a spirit does immediately after death. You used to own the night and put it to good use, during that sweet spot after your father could no longer tell you when to go to sleep and before you shared an apartment with someone else. Is togetherness killing your productivity? When's the last time you stayed up until 4:00 A.M. testing the boundaries of your consciousness and Googling serial killers?

But then you remember how hard it was, that moment between wakefulness and sleep. How the moment of settling down was almost physically painful, your mind pulling away from your body like a balloon being sucked into the atmosphere. He settles that. He tells you that your day was rich enough and now it is time to wind down. He helps you sleep. People need sleep.

You've learned a new rule and it's simple: don't put yourself in situations you'd like to run away from.

But when you run, run back to yourself, like that bunny in *Runaway Bunny* runs to its mother, but you are the mother, and you'll see that later and be very, very proud.

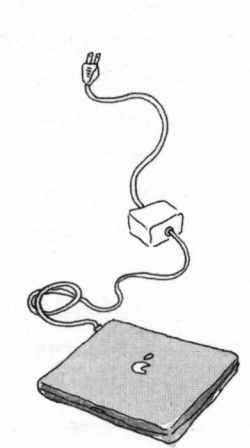

# *Acknowledgments*

I WOULD LIKE TO gratefully acknowledge the following people, who were instrumental in the writing and publication of this book:

Peter Benedek, the greatest friend and champion. I owe you so much, which is why I give you 10 percent of all my money. Jenny Maryasis, you are a most literary and forthright woman in a world full of dummies who lie. Thank you both.

Kimberly Witherspoon, thank you for encouraging me to take up all the space I need, both in a chair and on the page.

Jodi Gottlieb, who really keeps it classy.

Susan Kamil, Gina Centrello, and the rest of the Random House femme-squad. A beautiful bunch.

Andy Ward, you are the best editor a girl who uses the word "vagina" a lot could ever ask for. Your careful, attentive, and brilliant work on this book has had an impact far beyond these pages. Hi, Abby and Phoebe ☺.

David, Esther, and the whole Remnick/Fein clan: your friendship and wisdom have been a balm to my soul. Thank you for the endless humor, encouragement, and matzo brie.

Joana Avillez, you draw the world I wish to inhabit. This book is a document of our twenty-five-year friendship.

Ilene Landress, who keeps me going, keeps me on time, and makes me very happy

Jenni Konner: my best friend, my partner in work and crime. It's not a coincidence that shortly after I met you I stopped losing my voice. Every day, thank you. I love you, Mack and Coco!

My family: Your art, humor, and love are my reason. I'm sorry I keep doing this to you. Laurie and Tip, I'm done at least until you die. But Grace, you aren't off the hook quite yet.

Aunties SuSu and Bonmom, Grandma Dot, Uncle Jack, the cousins who are here and who are gone, Rick and Shira and Rachum.

Jack Michael Antonoff. These words would never exist if not for your love and support. Thank you for making a life and home with me.

Isabel Halley, Audrey Gelman, Jemima Kirke—friends and muses. The funniest and prettiest of them all.

A hearty thank-you to all the brassy folks I interact with every day on the Internet, who have supported my self-expression, challenged me plenty, and confirmed my ultimate hope that the world is full of kindreds.

I have received help, encouragement, and inspiration from many. This list includes, but is not limited to: Ericka Naegle, Mike Birbiglia, Leon Neyfakh, Alice Gregory, Miranda July, Delia Ephron, Ashley C. Ford, Paul Simms, Charlie McDowell and the Roon, Murray Miller, Sarah Heyward, Bruce Eric Kaplan, Judd Apatow, B. J. Novak, the *New Yorker* magazine, *Glamour* magazine, *Rookie* magazine, HBO, Mindy Kaling, Alicia Van Couvering, Matt Wolf and Carl Williamson, Teddy Blanks, Roberta Smith and Jerry Saltz, Taylor and all her songs, Polly Stenham, Larry Salz, Kassie Evashevski, Richard Shepard, David Sedaris, Zadie Smith, Tom Levine, Maria Santos, Ariel Levy, Kaela Myers, Maria Braeckel, Tom Perry, Theresa Zoro, Leigh Marchant, Erika Seyfried, and Lamby.

## ABOUT THE AUTHOR

LENA DUNHAM is the creator of the critically acclaimed HBO series *Girls,* for which she also serves as executive producer, writer, and director. She has been nominated for eight Emmy awards and has won two Golden Globes, including Best Actress, for her work on *Girls.* She was the first woman to win the Directors Guild of America award for directorial achievement in comedy. Dunham has also written and directed two feature-length films (including *Tiny Furniture* in 2011) and is a frequent contributor to *The New Yorker.* She lives and works in Brooklyn, New York.

## ABOUT THE TYPE

This book was set in Baskerville, a typeface designed by John Baskerville (1706–75), an amateur printer and typefounder, and cut for him by John Handy in 1750. The type became popular again when the Lanston Monotype Corporation of London revived the classic roman face in 1923. The Mergenthaler Linotype Company in England and the United States cut a version of Baskerville in 1931, making it one of the most widely used typefaces today.

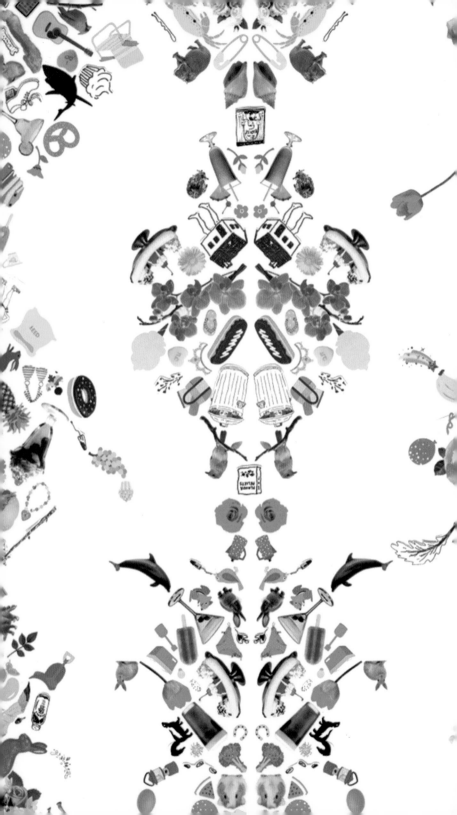